Creating TV Formats

Creating TV Formats: From Inception to Pitch takes the reader through a step-by-step process of how to generate ideas, develop story lines and characters and hook an audience, whilst staying aware of the realities of the media landscape.

Beginning with a discussion about what a TV format is, each chapter then introduces a key aspect of the development process, such as looking for ideas, shaping the underlying story and thinking about participants. Practical exercises guide the reader through each stage of turning an initial idea or subject matter into a hook or insight; the importance of incorporating storytelling principles and techniques for designing and populating a story world. Examples from successful television formats such as *First Dates* and *The Great British Bake Off* are interwoven throughout the book alongside exclusive insights from the key industry professionals who brought them to the screen.

From short-form digital content to longer unscripted series, this is an essential guide to discovering and developing formats for any media or television production student or early career development professional.

Catriona Miller, PhD, is a professor in Media at Glasgow Caledonian University, where she teaches on creativity and media content development. Her research interests include storytelling and the archetypal dimensions of science fiction, horror and fantasy genres, publishing her monograph *Cult TV Heroines* in 2020. She also publishes on Jungian film theory and co-edited *Exploring Depth Psychology and the Female Self: Feminist Views from Somewhere* with Leslie Gardner in 2021. She is a senior fellow of the Higher Education Academy.

Hazel Marshall is a writer, story trainer and consultant with a diverse background in the craft of shaping narratives across a wide range of factual genres and platforms. She ran popular, practical storytelling workshops for almost ten years at the BBC, training hundreds of programme makers in her time there. She continues to train production teams making series for multiple channels and streamers and has been a story or script consultant on numerous award-winning landmark series.

Linda Green is Founding Director of Leading Creative Talent helping to develop and sell formats in the UK and internationally, providing creative development and pitch coaching for major broadcasters and production companies. Prior to this, as Head of Creative Leadership at the BBC, Linda designed the BBC's Creative Leadership Programme which delivered new ideas and talent for the UK's top formats. Linda speaks regularly at industry events and has delivered creative ideas and leadership seminars for universities across Europe.

Creating TV Formats
From Inception to Pitch

Catriona Miller, Hazel Marshall and Linda Green

Routledge
Taylor & Francis Group
LONDON AND NEW YORK

Designed cover image: Illustration by Zoobs Ansari

First published 2023
by Routledge
4 Park Square, Milton Park, Abingdon, Oxon OX14 4RN

and by Routledge
605 Third Avenue, New York, NY 10158

Routledge is an imprint of the Taylor & Francis Group, an informa business

© 2023 Catriona Miller, Hazel Marshall and Linda Green

The right of Catriona Miller, Hazel Marshall and Linda Green to be identified as authors of this work has been asserted in accordance with sections 77 and 78 of the Copyright, Designs and Patents Act 1988.

All rights reserved. No part of this book may be reprinted or reproduced or utilised in any form or by any electronic, mechanical, or other means, now known or hereafter invented, including photocopying and recording, or in any information storage or retrieval system, without permission in writing from the publishers.

Trademark notice: Product or corporate names may be trademarks or registered trademarks, and are used only for identification and explanation without intent to infringe.

British Library Cataloguing-in-Publication Data
A catalogue record for this book is available from the British Library

Library of Congress Cataloging-in-Publication Data
Names: Miller, Catriona, 1968– author. | Marshall, Hazel, 1969– author. |
Green, Linda, 1973– author.
Title: Creating TV formats : from inception to pitch / Catriona Miller,
Hazel Marshall and Linda Green.
Description: Abingdon, Oxon ; New York, NY : Routledge, 2023. |
Includes bibliographical references.
Identifiers: LCCN 2022029166 | ISBN 9780367506513 (hardback) |
ISBN 9780367506506 (paperback) | ISBN 9781003050650 (ebook)
Subjects: LCSH: Television authorship–Vocational guidance–Great Britain |
Reality television programs–Production and direction–Vocational guidance–Great Britain
Classification: LCC PN1992.7.M56 C74 2023 | DDC 791.45/72–dc23
LC record available at https://lccn.loc.gov/2022029166

ISBN: 9780367506513 (hbk)
ISBN: 9780367506506 (pbk)
ISBN: 9781003050650 (ebk)

DOI: 10.4324/9781003050650

Typeset in Goudy
by Newgen Publishing UK

This book is dedicated to all those whose questions inspired us: the workshop participants, creative leaders, development teams, production teams and the media and journalism students at Glasgow Caledonian University and Norway's TV School, Lillehammer.

Contents

List of Illustrations   viii
Preface   ix
Acknowledgements   xii

1. What Is a Format?   1
2. Be Creative   12
3. Do Creative   24
4. Shape It   41
5. Build It   63
6. Design It   77
7. Populate It   91
8. Drive It   108
9. Get Out There!   126

Appendix   130
Index   133

Illustrations

Figures

1.1	Development Circle	2
8.1	Pitching Checklist	122

Tables

3.1	TEASER Grid	38
4.1	Common Competition Format Shapes	46
4.2	Common Change Format Shapes	50
4.3	Common Choice Format Shapes	52
8.1	What Are the Values That Drive You?	110
8.2	IWISHU	114

Preface

This book came about because all three of us, in various contexts, have been teaching in this area for years: Hazel and Linda for industry and Catriona for Higher Education. Then we met. It seemed to us that formats had become the backbone of the TV industry (broadcast and increasingly online and streaming services too), but there was no roadmap to creating them and that is what all three of us had been trying to formulate.

What the Book Doesn't Do

There is a fine line where development (hopefully) becomes issues of production management. This book tries to keep to the development of ideas, rather than the practicalities of making a show into a reality, though there are, of course, areas which cross over. For example, decisions about a show's filming device (location, studio sets, fixed rig or observational documentary style, etc.) might affect how the story of the format is told, and thus is reasonable to include in the development process. Several of our interviewees discussed the importance of a strong vision for a production crew, while at the same time stressing the importance of flexibility on floor and in post-production. We can't cover this whole process in one book, so we are concentrating on the "strong vision" part. In a similar vein, we don't delve deeply into issues of intellectual property, health and safety, duty of care to participants in any depth, rights clearances, budgets or diversity policies and many of the other practical considerations that go into making a show into a reality. We focus on idea generation and developing the strongest idea possible – because without a fully formed brilliant idea, you have nothing to take to the industry.

Formats, particularly the longer running ones, often have quite a tangled history in terms of versions, commissioning channels, production companies, not to mention the international versions and, in some cases, reboots. So, to keep things as clear as possible, we have endeavoured, to the best of our ability, to reference shows in terms of the UK versions, and in terms of the current owners and production companies or the owner at the time of last transmission. We also don't discuss formats which originated outwith the UK – or only in passing – for example, *Dragon's Den* (BBC Studios, 2005–present) and *The Masked Singer*

(Bandicoot, 2020–present) both of which originated in South Korea and have been very successful around the world, choosing to keep our focus on the success of many UK-originated formats. Our combined experience is brought together in this book, and our experience is in UK television formats so that is what the book focusses on, though as Chapter 1 explains, since the UK has been a leader in this field, we do this without apology.

What the Book Does Do

This book is our roadmap to creating successful TV formats, but these seemingly simple shows require a wide-ranging skillset to be able to create them successfully. Curiosity, a flexible mindset and imagination are all essential, but at the same time, you also need to know how to tell a story, understand audiences as well as the requirements and realities of the television industry. So, you need to be creative but within a practical context. You must dare to dream but keep your feet on the ground. It is a tricky balancing act but working your way through this book will help. This is a way of doing things based on those ideas that have been successful, but you will also start to develop an understanding of why some shows didn't work. Although we show where some ideas come from in academic terms, it will be practical and easy to use, building up advice, exercises and examples as we go, so that you are primed for success.

One of the difficulties of creative ideas generation is that it is often an intuitive and non-linear process. Although we have structured the book in a certain way, the truth is that the spark for an idea can come from anywhere, at any stage. It might start with very particular industry facing requirements: a need to reverse engineer a show to service the needs of a niche audience, or a "hero show" to embody a channel brand. Or it might be a more freeform insight springing from a news story, or even a daydream, which must then be tailored to attract a commissioner. The idea itself and then its development into a successful format is a dynamic process with a constant push/pull, expansion/contraction, proliferation/condensation where ideas are opened up (sky's the limit!) then focussed back-down into specific requirements.

We have conceptualised this as the Development Circle moving from how to be creative and have an idea, through to effective storytelling, world building and persuading others, but you will probably need to go back and forth, reworking any of the areas at any point. So, this isn't necessarily an obvious step-by-step forward progress to a logical conclusion, but rather a non-linear sequence and each idea will follow its own path. There are a lot of moving pieces in a format, and you might need to jump back or forward, or even side to side to get to the point where all the pieces happily align. Remaining flexible and emotionally resilient through this sometimes lengthy process is essential.

The chapters build up detail and advice on the issues, with examples along the way, exploring the skills and attitudes you need. We ask many questions in the exercises, and the point is not to answer "yes or no" quickly. The point of the questions is to take time to think through, imagine, evaluate the pros and cons of doing things one way or another. The Development Circle covers all the bases, and if you work through it (in whatever order, however many rotations it takes), it will bring you closer to a successful conclusion – a commissioned show!

We would like to thank everyone who took part in helping us create this book. Their insight and contributions were invaluable as they are all successful format creators, producers and commissioners working in the industry today. Any fault you have with any of the processes or theories in the book lie with us and not with them. This is our take on format development – it's not the only way to do it. Anyone who tells you there is only one way to do anything creative is wrong. But we hope you use this book in a way that serves your own process and needs and, in time, develop your own skills.

Catriona, Hazel and Linda

Catriona Miller, PhD, is a professor in Media at Glasgow Caledonian University, where she teaches on creativity and media content development. Her research interests include storytelling and the archetypal dimensions of science fiction, horror and fantasy genres, publishing her monograph *Cult TV Heroines* for Bloomsbury in 2020. She also publishes on Jungian film theory and co-edited *Exploring Depth Psychology and the Female Self: Feminist Views from Somewhere* with Leslie Gardner for Routledge in 2021. She is a senior fellow of the Higher Education Academy.

Hazel Marshall's interest in storytelling comes from her diverse background in the craft of shaping narratives across a wide range of factual genres across multiple platforms as well as a background in fiction and drama. She started in radio before designing and delivering story and script courses for factual television across the BBC for almost a decade. She continues to do this as a freelance story trainer and consultant working with production teams making series across multiple channels and streamers. She has trained hundreds, if not thousands, of factual programme and documentary makers at all stages in their careers across multiple genres and been a story consultant on numerous award-winning landmark series.

Linda Green graduated from the London School of Economics before joining the BBC. Linda developed a keen interest in how audiences can inspire new ideas and help reboot brands, working on top formats including *Top Gear* and *Strictly Come Dancing*. Linda designed the BBC's Creative Leadership Programme which developed new ideas and talent for big events such as the 2012 Digital Olympics and big brands like *Doctor Who*, for big international broadcasters and the industry's biggest independent producers, including Fremantle and Banijay. Linda is Founder and CEO of Leading Creative Talent, an idea development, coaching and training company, and she's excited that this book is a chance to share development and leadership techniques to support the success of future content makers.

Acknowledgements

With grateful thanks to all our contributors for sharing their time and expertise with us:

Nell Butler, Joint CEO of Riverdog Productions
Gerard Costello, Executive Producer, IWC Media
Stephen Lambert, Chief Executive, Studio Lambert
Richard McKerrow, CEO and Chief Creative Director, Love Productions
Ana de Moraes, Chief Creative Officer at MultiStory Media
Jonathan Meenagh, Television Development Consultant
Narinder Minhas, CEO Cardiff Productions
Kate Phillips, BBC Controller, Entertainment
Caroline Roseman, Director of Development, Fulwell 73 Productions

Unless otherwise attributed in the text, quotes are drawn from interviews carried out by the authors in 2021–2022.

Please Note

Formats, particularly the longer running ones, often have a complex history in terms of versions, commissioning channels, production companies, not to mention the international versions and in some cases reboots. So, to keep things as clear as possible and based on the information available, to the best of our ability we have referenced shows in terms of UK versions and in terms of the current owners and production companies, or the owner at the time of last transmission.

1 What Is a Format?

TV formats have a huge impact on people's lives. They are one of the most powerful forms of storytelling on our screens today. *The Great British Bake Off* (Love Productions, 2010–present) sent demand for butter soaring as the "Bake Off Effect" encouraged its audience to have a go (Campbell-Schmitt, 2017), whilst *Strictly Come Dancing* (BBC Studios, 2004–present) has been used as a tool to get people moving (Age UK, 2017). *RuPaul's Drag Race* (World of Wonder, 2009–present) gives us an insight into another world. *Tattoo Fixers* (Studio Lambert, 2015–2019) shows we all make mistakes – and that those mistakes can be rectified. Formats have become one of the ways we make sense of ourselves and the world, to dream of better things and of tolerating difference. They have also been big business for the television industry. Audiences like watching them, and the industry likes making them.

This chapter will introduce you to the concept of formats, starting with a little history and the business context because it is the business drivers that led to and sustain the format boom. We will be discussing formats primarily within the context of broadcast television, which is where they have had the biggest impact, but we are alert to the evolving nature of the media industries, and that formats are being adapted for streaming services and global online platforms of all kinds. There has been a lot of movement in the world of "smaller screen" viewing in terms of business practices, delivery technology and the content itself, but for the sake of speed, in this book when we say "TV", we extend it in the broadest possible sense to cover traditional linear broadcast television, all non-linear "on demand" streaming services such as AVOD, SVOD, TVOD (Advertising, Subscription and Transaction Video on Demand) and other online audio-visual offerings. It is clear that formats can and are being created for almost any media platform. So, what we offer here are the principles and practices of format creation which can be adapted for any media platform, but we do not go into any great detail about the platforms themselves.

Going in Circles?

The aim of this book is to help you come up with an idea, and then to help you develop that idea into workable content ready for pitching. The tricky thing is

DOI: 10.4324/9781003050650-1

that this process, which might loosely be called "development", is not a straightforward one, it isn't a linear one, or perhaps, even to some extent, a logical one. It is a process which relies on intuitions and hunches as much as shrewd reasoning, but that doesn't mean there aren't a fairly regular series of issues and processes that can make you better at it.

So, in each chapter, we present you with a series of examples, prompts and exercises designed to help you think about, firstly, how to have an idea, and then how to take it from a "top-line" idea to something closer to a workable show. This can be a big step where the devil really is in the detail and a lot can change. A top-line idea could be as simple as "a dating show that begins where a good date ends", for example *Naked Attraction* (Studio Lambert, 2016–present), but how that actually appears on screen moment to moment, taking in questions such as is there a presenter, what will the set look like, who are the participants, what is the tone, who is the audience, can be the difference between an entertaining and long-lasting format, and one that never gets commissioned. *Naked Attraction* has had nine series to date in the UK and nine international versions.

The exercises are not something that need a quick yes/no answer, rather they are intended to help you think about your idea, opening up possibilities with only the sky as the limit and then closing things down again as you take on-board real-world constraints that require flexible responses. Rather than an immediate answer you will probably need to keep asking questions, keep exploring and keep researching and work round the idea one more time. The processes, questions, provocations and exercises contained in the book might take you round in a big circle. That is why we call it the Development Circle (see Figure 1.1).

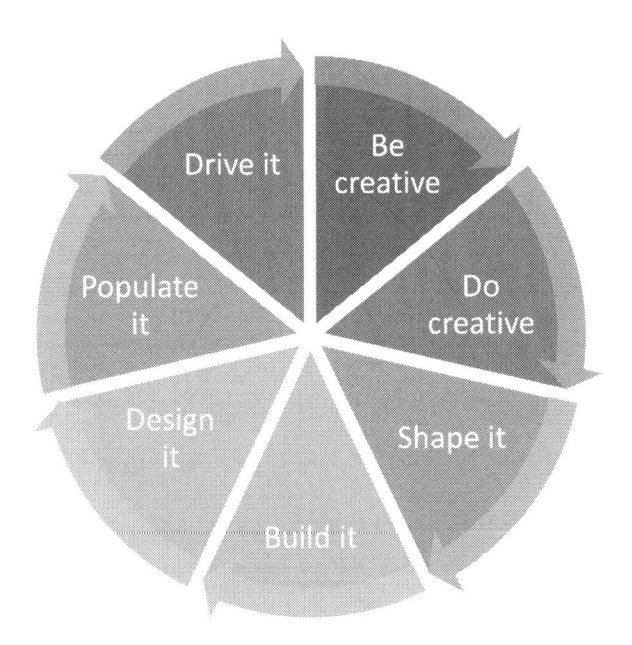

Figure 1.1 Development Circle

The truth is that the starting point could come anywhere in the circle. Sometimes the industry has a quite specific idea of what they need: a commissioner has a professional talent in mind they wish to find a vehicle for (casting), or a channel is looking for a show that will serve a specific audience (an insight), but often commissioners don't know exactly what they are looking for until they see it and production companies are always working on new ideas to pitch. For this book, however, we have to begin the circle somewhere and so after this introduction to the concept of formats, we begin with the practical question of creativity. As neuroscientist Dietrich put it, 'creativity is a complex and multifaceted construct that can manifest in a myriad of different ways' (Dietrich, 2019, p. 1), and we think it is so important that we devote two whole chapters to it because, without that first inkling of an idea, you don't have a show. We believe that everyone is creative, and that you can always get better at it, so we consider how to be a more creative person in Chapter 2 and then how to develop and deepen your creative process in Chapter 3. These two chapters will offer you some history and perspectives on how creativity has been understood, as well as practical exercises to get you ready to find your format idea.

The circle then moves on to deepening that initial idea, helping you transition from that good "top-line" concept to something with more detail. There are chapters on the type of story you might be trying to tell, the beats you will take, building the story world, design considerations, character and casting in Chapters 4–7, before taking a closer look at the people you may need to bring on board to help you and finishing with some tips on communicating your idea in Chapter 8.

This is unlikely to be a linear process for you. In fact, even saying it is a circle suggests a certain clear direction of travel, but we hope you will hold on to this idea of moving round a circle as you begin to see how many of these elements are interconnected and how challenging it can be to make sure that everything is working together. The goal is to tell a gripping story consistently week after week, for years on end (with any luck). So, we hope you will keep moving back and forth through the book as you adapt elements, sharpen focus and gradually bring everything into alignment. It can be done, and this book will help you to do it.

Why Do Formats Matter?

Audiences love formats, as shown by the long running nature of shows like *Masterchef* (Banijay 1990/2005–present). In the UK it has run every year since its reboot in 2005 (and that's not even counting celebrity or junior spin offs) and has been adapted for around 65 different countries. It is clear that if a format hits the right spot, longevity and wide reach around the globe are real possibilities. This makes formats a sound business proposition.

Formats have been around from the very early days of broadcasting, beginning with radio. The American radio show *It Pays to Be Ignorant* is a good contender for being the first ever format. The show began on CBS radio in 1942 but was then bought and adapted for BBC Radio's Light Programme in 1948 as *Ignorance Is Bliss*. However, during the 1960s, 1970s and 1980s, formats remained a relatively small part of the television industry, mostly focused on game shows. Two Australian companies, Fremantle and Reg Grundy, between them controlled the global rights to the Goodson-Todman catalogue, a US company formed in 1946 which was responsible for a string of hits such as *The Price Is Right* (1956), *Winner Takes All* (which began on radio in 1946 before moving to television in 1948), *What's My Line* (1950) and *Call my Bluff* (1965). These shows are all still distributed by Fremantle. *The Price Is Right* has been licenced in at least 47 countries over the years, so just to be clear, that is one intellectual property sold 47 times.

The US dominance of gameshows in terms of international sales continued until the 1980s. It wasn't until 1981 that, for the first time, a format was sold to the US from the UK, when *The Krypton Factor* (ITV Studios, 1977) was sold to American network ABC. *The Krypton Factor* was an early evening game show (the name referring to Superman's home planet of Krypton) where contestants put a range of skills and aptitudes to the test, including intelligence tests, observation rounds, general knowledge and what became a famous assault course to test their physical abilities. *The Krypton Factor* is significant because it was such a success that Granada (now part of ITV plc) stopped looking to America for its quiz shows and game show formats and began generating more of their own (Leahy, 2016). This was good news for UK TV, but the world of formats remained focused on the relatively niche area of gameshows until the1990s when the pace of change suddenly picked up. As Chalaby (2012) noted, it was in the 1990s that international TV trade flows which had been dominated by the sale of finished programmes began instead to look with fresh eyes at formats, where the outline of a show could be sold to be produced locally. The "format revolution" radically changed the nature of and volume of that trade, although it was a revolution, Chalaby points out, which had been 50 years in the making.

The 1990s saw the global television business going through several structural changes that had the effect of making the proposition of formats more and more attractive. Changes in technology and introduction of cable and satellite in the UK meant that there were more channels than ever before, compounded again in 2012 when the whole of the UK shifted to digital broadcasting. By and large these changes were mirrored across Europe, and globally television was also growing especially in BRICS countries (Brazil, Russia, India, China and South Africa).

More channels meant more broadcast hours which in turn required more content, but the trade in finished programmes wasn't hitting the spot for audiences who 'are understood to have a preference for programmes that are attuned to their sense of who they are' (Moran & Aveyard, 2014, p. 20). Suddenly, selling the outline of a show rather than the finished article was looking more appealing. Formats could be locally produced and tailored towards local tastes, but without the risks and expense of developing a completely new idea. There is a high failure rate in television, so buying-in an already proven format was seen as a potential shortcut to audience success. As one industry professional put it, 'a format has "been debugged" to remove the mistakes that have been made and won't be made again' (Chalaby, 2011, p. 295). Formats are also often capable of being produced in high volume thus reducing costs even further.

At the same time, however, there had also been changes in UK institutional frameworks with the UK government intent on "opening up" the TV industry to greater competition. Whereas previously the channels had created, produced and broadcast their own programmes, now the government made it a requirement that a certain proportion of content had to be commissioned from independent production companies. This led to a whole host of new companies being founded in the 1980s and 1990s, many of whom are now owned by bigger corporations: for example, Shed Media is now part of Warner Media; Tiger Aspect is part of Endemol, which is part of the Endemol Shine Group, which is now part of Banijay; though others like Hat Trick (founded in 1986) are still independent. Even the UK's biggest two public service broadcasters eventually got on board with the creation of ITV Studios and BBC Studios who make programmes for any customer not just their "home" channel.

A final piece of the puzzle fell into place with the 2003 Communications Act which established a more equitable distribution of the intellectual property associated with television programmes. Intellectual property for programmes can be loosely split into three areas. Primary rights – the right to broadcast the show, which usually lies with the commissioning channel. In other words, if you paid for it to be made, you get the right to show it first. Secondary rights, that is the rights to repeat showing of the same finished programme, and because of that growth in cable, satellite and then streaming services, the rights to repeats became much more valuable, and the independent production companies which had developed the shows in the first place wanted to be able to sell the programmes on to other buyers. Finally, there are tertiary rights related to ancillary branded merchandise like games, books, clothes, toys and even experiences.

The problem was that whilst the primary rights had certainly been the most valuable part of the supply chain (i.e. exclusive premieres), through the 1990s and into the 2000s, secondary and tertiary rights were fast growing in value too, but the broadcasters had 'either captured all the value of these rights for themselves under restrictive contracts or alternatively not bothered to exploit such rights, preventing a potential stream of revenue back to the original producer' (Haynes, 2005, p. 93). Channels had tended to "bundle rights" when they purchased shows, but after 2003 the independent production companies were able to make better deals for themselves and hang on to more of those rights for themselves.

For example, *Who Wants to Be a Millionaire* (Sony Pictures Television, 1998–present) was originally developed by the independent production company Celador, who realised that they should preserve as much IP as possible. As a result, they, rather than ITV, the channel who premiered it in 1998, were able to profit from the sales of board games, for example. This also meant that independent production companies could sell the rights to their shows into other territories or to look for other broadcasters. Hence Love Productions' freedom in 2017 to shift *The Great British Bake Off* from the BBC to Channel 4. So, by the late 1990s and early 2000s, as Chalaby put it, 'Trade figures exploded: the number of formats in circulation, the number of territories they travelled to, the number of companies involved and the volume and speed of business' (Chalaby, 2011, p. 298) – the format revolution had arrived.

The business case had been growing, but the form of TV formats was also evolving and moving away from the gameshow. In 2005, Peter Bazalgette, former Chief Creative Officer for Endemol, one of the architects of the TV format era in television, described the creation of what he called three "super formats" (Bazalgette, 2005): *Who Wants to Be a Millionaire; Survivor* (Banijay); and *Big Brother* (Banijay), to which Chalaby (2011) added *Pop Idol* (the 2001 UK show had a rather troubled history, but the *Idol* franchise is currently in the Fremantle catalogue).

Between them, these pioneering formats established a blend of straight-forward competition, fly on the wall observation, confessional cameras, individual stories of success, failure, high endeavour and transformation that have formed the core of so many of the formats that followed them. They also have proved to have far greater longevity than anyone could have predicted at the time with all these formats still going strong somewhere in the world.

What Is a Format?: Three Paradoxes

Up until now we have "talked around" the concept of formats without clearly defining what we mean by a format. This is because whilst the industry happily uses the term for a range of non-scripted factual and entertainment shows, there isn't in fact wide agreement about its definition.

We asked all our interviewees the question "what is a format?" and received quite a variety of answers. Some didn't much like definitions. Some thought it was real life but blown up into something bigger and magical. Others thought of it as a process of bringing change that would create drama, emotion and possibly comedy, or a structure that will always deliver emotional spikes along with a certain comfort and familiarity; or a form of people-watching the audience can relate to by putting someone into a situation and seeing how they get on with a few rules laid down by TV; or a set of rules that is reproducible with different casts and talent in different territories; or simply the distinctive set rules and structures you put on an idea; or a programme that is repeatable and has a sense of regularity about it.

The word format is more modern than you might suppose. Although it has its origins in a Latin phrase – *(Liber) formatus* (meaning "a book formed") – which does seem to suggest a certain antiquity – in fact it is modern Latin and only dates from 1840. It comes from the past participle of *formare* "to form" from *forma* meaning form, or shape. One suggestion is that it works its way into modern usage through its adoption in the early world of computer programming by 1955. However, the *Oxford English Dictionary* cites *The Spectator* magazine of 1958 – 'The principle performer... had to write the scripts herself and when... she attempted to heed criticism and alter the format, she was told that the show, however bad, must go on' (Moran & Malbon, 2006, p. 19–20).

Academia has tried to analyse formats in a variety of ways, though the discussion often drifts towards the question of genre, but this creates a new problem because the concept of "genre" itself is complicated within a cultural context. The term "genre" is derived from a scientific model of classifying objects based on their similarity and difference to other objects, but the association with scientific principles is misleading because it assumes that these 'classifications are like standards: formalised, durable rules which extend over several communities of practise' (Frow, 2015, p. 56–57). When attempting to find such durable rules for cultural objects like television programmes, problems emerge because programmes exist in a structure more like a family tree than in neat boxes.

A good example of this kind of genre fuzziness was *Faking It* (RDF Media/Channel 4, 2000–2006). It was one of the earliest factual entertainment formats and began in the same year as *Big Brother* premiered in the UK. (*Big Brother* had launched the previous year in the Netherlands). *Faking It* was a huge success and ran for nine seasons in the UK (48 episodes). Stephen Lambert, who created the show for RDF Media, made it clear that 'the show uses documentary techniques to entertain and enlighten the viewer as well as sending the protagonists on a personal journey' (Gibson, 2006) and in the same article called it a 'formatted documentary' admitting it was 'creating a situation rather than documenting'. Indeed, as one writer pointed out 'every episode follows the same formula, and even the jury at Montreaux [who awarded it the Rose d'Or in 2003] commended it for its drama rather than realism' (Morreale in Heller, 2007, p. 98). Was it factual documentary, or some kind of manufactured entertainment?

Faking It was, of course, a bit of both, introducing a hybridity to the genre that has since been adopted many times over by Lambert himself with shows such as *Wife Swap* (RDF Media, 2003–2009, 2017), *Undercover Boss* (Studio Lambert, 2009–2014, but the show is still in production in the US,), *Gogglebox* (Studio Lambert, 2013–present), *Race Across the World* (Studio Lambert, 2019–present) and *The Circle* (Studio Lambert, 2018–2021, but again a US version is still in production for Netflix). 'What people call "populist rubbish"', Lambert said some years later in 2015, 'is just about the hardest thing to make. It's a million times easier to make some obscure documentary than to make something really good and accessible that will hold people's attention over many episodes' (Lambert, 2015).

In 2006, Moran and Malbon suggested that the term format implied that something can be copied from a core or structuring centre, a kind of cooking recipe where 'a television format is understood as that set of invariable elements in a programme out of which the variable elements of an individual episode are produced' (Moran & Malbon, 2006, p. 20). In 2007, Hill reconsidered genre and suggested that there had been a shift towards two kinds of format: competitions and factual entertainment, which introduced an element of fly-on-the-wall documentary to what was now called Reality TV, but also drew distinction between shows that had been specifically set up for the camera and those which were already taking place (Hill, 2007, p. 49). Chalaby played up the narrative element in 2011, suggesting 'a format is a show that can generate a distinctive narrative and is licenced outside its country of origin in order to be adapted to local audiences'

8 What Is a Format?

(Chalaby, 2011, p. 296). Whilst in 2014 Moran and Aveyard expanded their definition beyond narrative saying it was a template, 'a set of franchised knowledge and services, [which] distils the experiences and skills of the programme's original creators and allows the programme to be adapted and produced for broadcast in other territories' (Moran & Aveyard, 2014, p. 18).

All these definitions, and the example of *Faking It*, bring into focus one of the most important points about a format – there is always an element of artifice. Of course, all audio-visual texts present a *version* of reality (even documentary), one that has been "worked upon" to some extent in selection and editing decisions, but formats take things further and introduce rules and interventions on the "reality" within which the participants exist, and thus constrains to varying degrees how they must behave.

In fact, both the academic perspective and the industry perspective can be summed up in three paradoxes which lie at the heart of formats: they are real, but not real; each episode is the same but different, and they are local but can also be readily adapted for international markets. The artifice, the setup, the constraints in formats are there to ensure that *every* episode will reliably, simply and repeatedly generate stories, whilst leaving space for real people to have real experiences, reactions and emotions. The clarity of these rules means that formats are readily adaptable to a wide range of international markets, whilst remaining recognisably the same. The ability of formats to reliably deliver entertaining content means they are also "scalable", that is they can be produced in high volume and lend themselves to returning series. For example, the property finding format *Location, Location, Location* (IWC Media, 2000–present) has been on UK television screens for over 20 years with 37 series to date.

So, we define a format as a constructed reality which uses a predetermined set of rules to create recognisable, repeatable and scalable stories. This means that:

- A format is generative not just descriptive – the predetermined set of rules constructs reality in such a way as to guarantee a story (*real but not real*).
- A format lends itself to repetition without replication, by bringing real people into the constructed reality (*the same but different*, i.e. the setup is the same, but the people are different).
- A format is predisposed to easy adaptation because the constructed reality can be transplanted to many different locations with minimal changes (*local but global*).

The Development Circle will take you through two of these paradoxes at various points. For example, Chapter 5 explores the "real but not real" aspects of constructing a story world and Chapter 7 explores the "same but different" paradox in terms of your potential story world participants, but the third "global but local" paradox lies out with the scope of this book, as it relates to a (hopefully) later process of adapting a format for international markets. It is, however, worth keeping this potential future development in mind as you work though some of the questions and exercises: what could change and what would need to stay the same to keep the format intact?

A Good Story

This book is designed to help you get better at generating ideas, and then to help you navigate those paradoxes at the heart of formats so that you can construct a reality that will guarantee good stories time after time. At their heart formats really are very simple stories – arguably the simpler the better and where the hook of the story is often in the title – *The Great British Bake Off*, *Race Across the World*, *Who Wants to Be a Millionaire*. But saying something is simple doesn't mean it is simple to make – "simple but good" is one of the hardest things to pull off. Your format might have a twist in it (as many good stories do) but it must be clear and easily explained, not like the episode in *Friends* (8.20) *The One with the Baby Shower* (Bright/Kauffman/Crane Productions, Warner Bros. Television, 2002) where Joey (Matt LeBlanc) auditions to be the host for "Bamboozled" – a game show so complicated *no one* can understand it.

In Chapter 4 we set out what we think some of the most successful story types are based on three larger categories: Competition formats, Change formats and Choice formats. This classification is not intended to work as a set of genre rules, but rather a tool to help you focus on the *story* of your idea, which in turn will help you figure out the rules needed to propel that story forward. And in Chapter 7 we ask you to think about the characters, that is the participants, or contestants who will enact your story, characters who will have a desire for something – to win, to find love, to challenge themselves in some way. Those predictable, repeatable elements of a format's "predetermined set of rules" are the key to creating stories in episode after episode, although the story must always balance between the expected and the unexpected ("the same but different"). There is joy in familiarity – we often know what is going to happen, we just don't know how. Every makeover is different because the people being made over have different back stories and so we don't know how it will play out. From *Queer Eye* (Scout Productions, 2018–present) to *Sort Your Life Out with Stacey Solomon* (Optomen Productions, 2021–present), it is the constant stream of different characters who want to change that keep us watching.

Formats have a clearly defined story world which we explore in Chapter 6, and we know where we are when we see it, for example, *Strictly Come Dancing* is all bright colours and sparkle, whilst *Masterchef* (Banijay, 1990/2005–present) focuses on a more monotone world of clean crisp chef whites and stainless-steel surfaces, so Chapter 6 also explores how design helps to construct the reality of the world in which your story and characters are operating. This is a strong identifying aspect of a format but paradoxically it is one of the easiest things which can be tweaked whenever a format travels to another country – in Brazil, *Come Dine with Me* (ITV Studios, 2005–present) has a presenter and a parrot, whilst the French version eliminates the sarky voiceover provided in the UK version by Dave Lamb (Thomas, 2017) thus demonstrating the "local but global" paradox.

Exercise: Getting Your Eye In

Begin with your own viewing habits. What is your favourite format? (Wait… what do you mean you don't have one! Oh, right, there are too many to choose from. Phew! Because if you don't watch and love formats, it's going to be *really* difficult to develop one.)

The task is to observe what is on the screen for your chosen format, and then start to break it down into its constituent parts because all these elements are the result of creative decisions. The general tone, design and content must work with the casting and structure to create the right mood and feel with a great story keeping you gripped till the last minute. The more you can recognise these elements in formats that already exist and which work, the easier you will find it to start developing your own format.

Try to answer the following questions. Jot down your thoughts as you go, and you will start to create an outline of a format that works:

- What does it look and sound like? In terms of setting, colours, music and so on. *Really* look at the setting, the background, the opening shots, the closing shots.
- Who is on-screen? Are there presenters, judges, participants, contestants, experts, the public, even a voice over or a narrator?
- How is it structured? What is happening? Are there tasks, interviews, live elements, on location? What happens and how much of it at a time?
- What is the jeopardy? What is at stake? Where is the climax of the show?
- How would you characterise it overall? Is it lively and upbeat, fast paced? Or something gentler, and more fluid? Describe it in at least three adjectives.
- Can you compare it to other similar formats and figure out what makes them different from each other?
- Then maybe try one that you think *doesn't* work so well. Or, at least, since personal taste comes into this – one that doesn't intrigue you as much as some others. We would even challenge you to watch one in an area that you aren't interested in and see what pulls you in – or doesn't.

This book will take you round the Development Circle, asking you questions, setting you tasks and exercises, discussing how some of the most successful formats build their worlds, their stories and their characters, to help you navigate the paradoxes at the heart of format development. And we begin in the next chapter with some discussion about creativity and how to start deepening and strengthening your own.

References

Age UK, 2017, Reasons for Older People to Join a Dance Class, *Age Co*. Retrieved April 24, 2022, from www.ageukmobility.co.uk/mobility-news/article/reasons-older-people-join-dance-class/

Bazalgette, P., 2005, *Billion Dollar Game: How 3 Men Risked It All and Changed the Face of TV*, St Ives, Time Warner Books.

Campbell-Schmitt, A., 2017, Global Butter Prices Are Rising Like Crazy, *Food & Wine*, Retrieved May 2, 2022, from www.foodandwine.com/news/butter-prices-rising-2017

Chalaby, J., 2011, The Making of an Entertainment Revolution: How the TV Format Trade Became a Global Industry, *European Journal of Communication*, 26(4), pp. 293–309.

Chalaby, J., 2012, At the Origin of a Global Industry: The TV Format Trade as an Anglo-American Invention, *Media, Culture and Society*, 34(1), pp. 36–52.

Dietrich, A., 2019, Types of Creativity, *Psychonomic Bulletin & Review*, 26, pp. 1–12.

Frow, J., 2015, *Genre*, Abingdon, Routledge.

Gibson, O., 2006, Making It, Not Faking It, *The Guardian*, Retrieved May 2, 2022, from www.theguardian.com/media/2006/oct/23/independentproductioncompanies.mondaymediasection

Haynes, R., 2005, *Media Rights and Intellectual Property*, Edinburgh, Edinburgh University Press.

Hill, A., 2007, *Restyling Factual TV: Audiences and News, Documentary and Reality Genres*, Abingdon, Routledge.

Lambert, S., 2015, Interviewed by A. McElvoy for the Royal Television Society, July 2, Retrieved May 2, 2022, from https://rts.org.uk/article/stephen-lambert-revolutionising-television

Leahy, Steve, 2016, Steve Leahy on the creation of The Krypton Factor, *Granadaland.org*. Retrieved April 23, 2022, from www.granadaland.org/steve-leahy-on-the-creation-of-the-krypton-factor/

Moran, A. & Aveyard, K., 2014, The Place of Television Programme Formats, *Continuum: Journal of Media & Cultural Studies*, 28(1), pp. 18–27.

Moran, A. & Malbon, J., 2006, *Understanding the Global TV Format*, Bristol, Intellect Books, p.19–20.

Morreale, J. 2007, Faking It and the Transformation of Personal Identity, in D. Heller (ed), *Makeover Television: Realities Remodelled*, London, I B Tauris, pp. 95–106.

Thomas, D., 2017, How to Turn a Hit TV Show into an International Success, bbc.co.uk. Retrieved May 2, 2022, from www.bbc.co.uk/news/business-40301134

2 Be Creative

In the introduction we proposed the concept of the Development Circle as an on-going process where an idea can be worked on and developed to focus and refine it, but that does mean, of course, that there must be an idea to work on in the first place. So, how do you start? Where do ideas come from? Increasingly, creativity is talked about and championed as an important quality or skill that we all need to have, but creativity itself can be an elusive concept and Chapters 2 and 3 will help you think about that creative spark from two related areas: "being creative" and "doing creative".

This chapter will introduce the concept of creativity with a little historical context, before moving on to a psychological perspective, whilst offering some practical suggestions along the way to help you think about your own creativity. Then Chapter 3 will offer a more externally facing focus on creativity as a process. You may already feel you have an inclination towards one of these perspectives rather than the other but thinking about creativity from both viewpoints will help to boost your creative potential. You will find that this chapter doesn't discuss formats, or even television, because it is focussing on you, and your creative potential. This is where the journey must begin.

What Is Creativity?

The origin of the word "creativity" stems from the Latin verb *ceare*, meaning to bring forth, to make or produce something. This suggests a "something from nothing", or a Big Bang sort of a moment, which was originally understood as divine in nature. Indeed, for many centuries, in Europe at least, 'the idea of "creation" was associated with God and the generative powers of nature' (Glăveanu & Kaufman, 2019, p. 10). The Renaissance marked the beginning of a long transition from creativity as the sole preserve of divinity towards something human beings could do, though by the early modern period it was still only very special, rare geniuses who were thought capable of it. These were artists and inventors who did what we might now call Creativity with a Big "C". However, over the course of the 19th and 20th centuries the idea of creativity underwent another shift, moving from a special ability that only a few people had towards a fundamental trait innate in all human beings. This has been called creativity with a little "c".

The reasons why this slow shift might have happened are complex, but in Europe there were two cultural changes weaving together. On the one hand the rise of rationality and the Scientific Method were developing through the Enlightenment, but at the same time artists and writers began exploring "irrational" sensibilities and personal emotion, with an interest in individual imagination and fantasy as never before. Artistic endeavour itself was shifting from an effort to represent the world in as realistic fashion as possible – a mimetic approach to art epitomised in the work of the Dutch Old Masters such as Johannes Vermeer (1632–1675) with their almost photographic paintings – towards a representation of an individual's *inner* world, explored by the Romantic poets such as Lord Byron (1788–1824) and artists like Caspar David Friedrich (1774–1840).

By the 20th century, these strands seem to culminate in a growing effort to understand the creative drive of great innovators, with creativity and the imagination being investigated *using* the tools of the scientific method. Graham Wallas (1858–1932), whose important book *The Art of Thought* (1926), we'll come back to in Chapter 3, was a psychologist who carried out some of the earliest theoretical work on creativity. However, his insights grew from previous research by Hermann von Helmholtz (1821–1894), a physicist and a physiologist, and Henri Poincaré (1854–1912), a mathematician. Science and the imagination were coming together, and the work of Wallas and others was shifting the understanding of creativity towards a process available to everyone rather than an innate talent only given to a few.

However, the idea that creativity belongs only to a few special people has proved to be a persistent one, even in the 21st century, because a strong research strand continued to focus on trying to discover the personal traits that these supposed creative geniuses had in common. This kind of research tended to culminate in lists which included things like (see Plucker et al, 2019, p. 10): awareness of creativity, originality, independence, risk taking, personal energy, curiosity, attraction to complexity and novelty, humour (though honestly when is that *not* good to have?), artistic sense, open-mindedness and so on. These traits are certainly important, but it does seem to make the discussion rather circular, taking us back to that idea of creativity with a Big "C" that somehow these are innate qualities that you either just have, or you don't.

Some researchers have tried to open up discussion further by proposing a Four C model (Kauffman & Beghetto, 2009) where Big-C and Pro-C refer to high-level and professional types of creativity, whilst little-c refers to an everyday creativity and mini-c 'captures the small acts of insight, wit, mental restructuring, imagination and improvisation in daily life' (Cotter et al, 2019, p. 641). The interesting thing is that this model can be applied in a developmental way meaning that practice with mini-c and little-c types of creativity will help you develop Pro-C and even Big-C creativity (see Kapoor & Kaufman, 2022). Those first two are particularly worth paying attention to, *especially* if you still think you are not a creative person, and perhaps an analogy can help us with this point. If we consider the quality of physical fitness, well, not everyone is cut out to be sporting professional, but we can all get fitter if we work out or do a form of exercise that suits us.

The Ancient Greek Temple of Delphi, whose origins go back to about 1500 BCE, had three aphorisms (or sayings) carved in its forecourt, "nothing to excess" was one, "surety brings ruin" another and third was the instruction "know yourself". On the whole still useful advice for today, but the last one is the key for us here. Knowing yourself is a lifelong task. Getting to know your own inner world and being confident in your own unique perspective on the world is worth the effort because there is no doubt the true source of creativity is your own inner psychological ecosystem. And the answer to the question, "where do ideas come from", is always ultimately *you*.

Getting to Know You: Some Insights from Jungian Psychology

Although there are many different approaches to the inner world of the psyche, concepts developed by one particular psychologist often crop up in discussions about creativity: the work of Swiss psychologist Carl Jung (1875–1961). For example, JP Guilford's concepts of convergent and divergent thinking, discussed in Chapter 3, are not dissimilar to Jung's ideas about directed and non-directed thinking originally published in 1912. Jung's theory was intrinsically influenced with his own creative practice (see *The Foundation of the Works of CG Jung*, 2018) and his influence on the origins of art therapy has been well documented (see Swan-Foster, 2020). That Jung's work is not more widely known in this context is largely the result of the professional and personal rift that grew between Sigmund Freud (1856–1939) and Jung after 1913, with the academic establishment tending to favour Freud through the influence of Jacques Lacan (1901–1981).

Jung was certainly creative in his theories and his artistic practice, and he thought that creativity was a human instinct as fundamental as hunger (Hillman, 1999, p. 31, quoting from a seminar conducted by Jung in 1936), but we don't introduce his ideas here as some kind of absolute truth. Rather they are intended as a model, or perhaps even better, a metaphor, for exploring your own inner world or psyche, which is Greek for "breath, life or soul" and is used to mean the inner world that psychology tries to investigate. Jung's own interests meant that his view of the psyche is one that remains well suited to considerations of creativity.

Although Jung himself didn't use this analogy, the totality of psyche can be thought of as a kind of ecosystem, where different regions work together to produce self-awareness and consciousness. For Jung, all parts of the psyche are valuable, including the unconscious which remains an active participant in the psyche, rather than being simply a repository of repressed contents, a kind of storage area for forgotten things, which is more like Freud's idea of the unconscious. The image of the ecosystem is useful – a tree, perhaps – because it is a system constantly in motion, all the elements working together, and the root system (the unconscious) is as large and as important as the visible canopy of leaves (the conscious). Jung certainly understood the psyche as a dynamic self-balancing system, more or less stable, but always in motion, always changing, very much like the contemporary understanding of an ecosystem.

At the simplest level, the psyche from Jung's perspective consists of conscious elements (that we are directly aware of) and unconscious elements (that we are not directly aware of, but which still have an effect on us). So, let's explore each of these two regions in turn because they both have a valuable role to play in creative activities.

The Conscious and Jungian Typology

When we think about ourselves, the thing we think of as "I", or when we say "me", is what Jung called the ego. This is the most conscious and self-aware part of the psychic ecosystem. We like to think that the ego is in charge, and most of the time it is, more or less, but it is intimately connected with the whole psyche, and sometimes it isn't quite as "in charge" as we like to imagine. The ego's job is to bring everything together: it orients basic attitudes and functions that Jung explored as types of consciousness. Sometimes this has been taken to mean personality types, but in fact Jung was talking about the different kinds of *consciousness* that we all have. We all have all of them available to us, though we will tend towards making use of some more than others but 'Jung was interested in illustrating how consciousness works in practice, and also in explaining how it is that consciousness works in different ways in different people' (Samuels et al, 1991, p. 153). We all have habits of thought but being aware of these habits gives you the ability to access or develop other ways of doing things, and in Chapter 3 we'll come back to the importance of breaking away from habitual ways of thinking for the creative process.

In terms of types of consciousness, Jung describes two attitudes and four functions, which we will very briefly explore – for more detail see Sharp (1987) or Beebe (2017).

The two attitudes are introvert and extrovert which are terms Jung coined. These are modes of adaptation and refer to whether you naturally, typically, relate more easily and frequently to the external world around you or to the internal psychological world.

- The extrovert looks outward. The introvert looks inward.
- The extrovert adapts easily and is accommodating. The introvert is slower to adapt and less changeable.
- The extrovert gains energy from new people, places, so tends to have many friends and acquaintances. The introvert loses energy to people and new situations, so tends to have fewer more intimate friendships.
- The extrovert might think introverts are boring and predictable. The introvert might think extroverts are flighty and superficial.

These are not absolutes and can shift depending on mood and situation, but perhaps you can recognise a more fundamental attitude that is more normal for you. If you are keen to get to the creative processes of Chapter 3, then perhaps you tend more towards the extrovert pole. The key point for us in the context of creativity is not that one is better than the other, but that having a sense of your more typical way of functioning might tell you what you could get better at. The extrovert might need to work on focus and deepening engagement with one thing. The introvert might need to work on being open to new things and staying curious.

So that's the two personality attitudes, but what about the four functions? These are thinking; sensation; feeling and intuition, but Jung had particular ideas in mind for each of these that might not be immediately obvious.

- Thinking refers to "the process of cognitive thought"; knowing what a thing is, naming it and linking it to other things. Sustained intellectuality, systematic thinking.
- Sensation is perception by means of the physical sense organs: sensation represents all facts available to the senses, telling us that something is, but not *what* it is. All the things you experience through your body. This is perceiving oriented to the external world.
- Feeling – by feeling, Jung does not (confusingly!) mean emotion, which psychologists are more likely to call affect. Instead, this is a consideration of the subjective *value* of something or having a viewpoint or perspective on something. Suppose someone says "Let's go to the beach! How do you feel about that?" Unless there's something unusual going on, you're unlikely to feel a sudden rage about the prospect, but you will have a perspective on whether that is something you'd be keen to do, or not. It might be quite a logical thing. "No, it's raining today, therefore I don't want to go to the beach". Or "Yes, I don't care if it is raining, I want to feel the sand between my toes". So feeling is the function of subjective judgement or valuation referring 'strictly to the way in which we subjectively evaluate what something, or someone, is worth to us' (Sharp, 1987, p. 17).
- Intuition – a sense of where something is going, of what the possibilities are, without conscious proof or knowledge. This is perceiving oriented to the internal world. Sometimes you just have a hunch about something!

Thinking and Feeling are considered "judging" functions; whilst Sensation and Intuition are "perceiving" functions and perhaps you can already see that *all four* of these types of conscious thinking are important to creative work. To be intuitive, to be open to the senses, helps to generate ideas, but also to be able to evaluate and judge their usefulness is equally essential. In fact, the point of Jung's typology is that all four should be valued equally, even though

> In practice the four functions are not equally at one's conscious disposal; that is, they are not uniformly developed or differentiated [in each of us].

Invariably one or the other is more developed, called the primary or superior function, while the rest remain inferior, relatively undifferentiated.

(Sharp, 1987, p. 15)

There are a great many sources dedicated to exploring these modes of conscious thinking in more detail, and there are many more online "personality tests" based on the Myers-Briggs test, for example. The Myers-Briggs test was developed from Jung's work, by mother and daughter Katharine Cook Briggs and Isabel Briggs Myers, and whilst there are plenty of critiques of the test, it can be an interesting tool for reflection. However, it is important *not* to use the test to put yourself into a box and regard it as the final word on the matter. Remember that we are thinking of the psyche as an ecosystem, and an ecosystem requires all parts to work together, growing in balance. We have access to *all* the types of conscious thinking Jung described, and to improve our creativity we might try to work on those areas we're less good at. Are you a bit too keen to close down exploration and jump to the "logical conclusion"? Then perhaps staying open to further ideas and embracing sensation or intuition might be important. Or do intuitions come to you, but you have trouble explaining yourself, in which case developing the systematic aspects of your thought might be worth investing in. Taking some time to consider what your habitual models of thinking might be and then working to develop those less available ways of thinking will be invaluable.

However, the conscious is only half of the Jungian model of the psyche, and although mostly hidden from our own view, the unconscious is also a vital part of the psychic ecosystem.

The Jungian Unconscious

Jung's idea of the unconscious was split into two areas. A personal unconscious, that contains repressed ideas, thoughts and memories, and another more fundamental layer, a region of the psyche where the possibility of consciousness begins in a psychic process which leads to ego formation and self-awareness. It was a deep region of the psyche which cannot ever become conscious. He called this the collective unconscious. It has been much discussed and critiqued, along with his idea of archetypes (patterns of psychic energy, which also can never become conscious). However, the important thing here is that for Jung, the unconscious is an active participant in the workings of the psyche, and that whilst it cannot be directly accessed, it can be indirectly worked with. This is where things can get interesting from a creativity point of view because the unconscious, if given some attention, can enhance our imagination and vision.

Through much of the history of humanity, Jung thought effort had been aimed at developing the capacity of the conscious to handle logical thought, but this came at the cost of the ability to listen to the unconscious. This led, in his opinion, towards one-sidedness. As he pointed out:

> The definiteness and directedness of the conscious mind are extremely important acquisitions which humanity has bought at a very heavy sacrifice, and which in turn have rendered humanity the highest service. Without them science, technology, and civilisation would be impossible.
>
> (Jung, 1960, pp. 69–70)

But, from this point of view, being conscious, self-aware creatures means that we have hidden away part of our psyche, but it isn't, as it were, switched off. It still functions below the waterline of consciousness and can make us behave in strange ways if we don't take care, but from a creativity point of view, the unconscious can be a catalyst for fertile imagination. To Jung's way of thinking, the ability to listen to your unconscious self is innate, it is just that you learn to discount it.

Now dreams are probably the most direct route to the unconscious, but Jung thought that they are often difficult to understand, so he also allowed for a more conscious creation and engagement with fantasy material through a process he call "active imagination". He thought that "spontaneous fantasies" are "more composed and coherent" than dreams and contain much that is "obviously significant" (Jung, 1960, p. 78). This is not conscious creation, but a spontaneous fantasy, or daydreaming and could be approached, he thought, not intellectually, but creatively by giving it a visible shape through painting or drawing, sculpture and even physically through bodily movements (Schaverien, 2005, p. 128).

Through this process of "active imagination" Jung saw the unconscious being brought into a more tangible form that could be apprehended by the conscious mind. The drama that manifests from the spontaneous fantasy appears to want to compel the viewer's participation (Jung, 1963, p. 496). A new situation is created in which unconscious contents are exposed to the waking state. Of course, for Jung, this process was intended to aid in psychic good health, but it is also the case that creativity can be enhanced by focussing on your inner world; perhaps even engaging with your unconscious self through daydreaming or certain creative activities, which will allow you to bring something from your inner world into first your own consciousness, and then perhaps into the external world to share with others.

The point of all this is to offer you a model or a metaphor to enhance your own creativity by understanding your own inner self better. You could consider Jung's typology with regard to your conscious ways of functioning, even if it is only so far as the attitudes of introversion or extroversion. What is your typical way of doing things? What if you tried something else? Then perhaps you can also start to give attention to some of your unconscious ways of functioning too, perhaps through thinking about your dreams more, or through active imagination activities, which could be a simple act of recording those mini-c activities mentioned earlier, those 'small acts of insight, wit, mental restructuring, imagination and improvisation in daily life' (Cotter et al, 2019, p. 641). Do you carry a notebook of some kind? Maybe this is the time to start!

But What about the Brain?

In this chapter we have begun our thinking about creativity from a psychological perspective, using Jung's model of the psyche as a metaphor for an inner ecosystem. This wasn't intended as an explanation of what creativity is, but rather a kind of imperfect map to different parts of your internal world, where recognising familiar pathways and less familiar pathways might help you to engage different parts of your own potential creativity. However, by this point you may be thinking that surely there must be a more "scientific" way of understanding creativity. What about the brain? What about neuroscience?

There is no doubt there has been a great deal of research carried out around the subject of creativity and the brain. The 1990s have been called the "decade of the brain" when the 'burgeoning field of neuroscience opened up to creativity studies' (Matthews & Nalbantian, 2019, p. 5). This kind of research has fallen into two waves so far. The first wave dating from the 1990s was looking for anatomical areas of the brain that might function in relation to creativity. However, the conclusion had to be reluctantly reached that, despite the initial excitement around left brain/right brain activities, 'no hemisphere or single brain region plays a leading role in creativity' (Vartanian, 2019, p. 155). There wasn't a part of the brain that researchers could point to as the source of creativity. As one writer put it

> From all we know about brain organisation, it is difficult to conceive of creativity, in all its shapes and forms, as emerging from a small common set of brain networks or as depending on a limited number of mental processes that have a distinct neural signature.
>
> (Dietrich, 2015, p. 37)

So, the second wave, like other aspects of neuroscience research, moved towards investigating creativity as a "completely distributed and fully embedded" phenomenon and exploring the network dynamics in the brain in line with the large-scale brain networks that emerged from other avenues of research. This approach showed that different areas of the brain *collaborate* in networks where 'The brain's large-scale functional networks apply organised effects on cortical areas, subcortical brain structures and effector organs during a variety of neurocognitive functions' (Parsons, 2017, p. 11).

There are three large-scale networks that are generally agreed upon. The central executive network which handles sustained attention, complex problem solving and working memory; the default mode network 'is associated with spontaneous and self-generated thought, and is typically observed when the person is not instructed to engage in a task' (Vartanian, 2019, p. 156). The third is the salience network which is less well understood but seems to play a role in mediating between the other two modes as appropriate. The default mode network has been particularly explored with a view to creativity.

However, part of the issue for neuroscience has been that there is no generally accepted definition of creativity to aid in their search. Typically divergent thinking (see Chapter 3) has been used as a proxy for creativity, but it is an imperfect one at best, and there has been a growing acceptance that creativity is a complex, composite thing and that until the sub-processes that make up the composite are better understood, the 'lack of a clear and detailed conceptual understanding of the construct of creativity leaves the field with no viable empirical paradigm to study its cognitive and neural mechanisms' (Dietrich, 2019, p. 3).

For us, from a practical perspective, however, there *are* still some insights to be drawn from all this. Dietrich (2019) makes a bid for three types of creativity which mirrors the large-scale brain networks more broadly:

- The deliberate mode associated with conscious processing, feelings of agency, executive or top-down attention, effort, volitional control, purposeful memory retrieval, intentionality and planning.
- The spontaneous mode associated with unconscious processing, no sense of agency, inattention or bottom-up attention, no volitional control, effortlessness, undirected memory retrieval and the eventual representation of the insight in working memory as surprising, intuitive and accidental.
- The flow mode when one becomes so deeply focused on a task and pursues it with such passion that all else disappears, including the passage of time. He associates flow specifically with movement of some kind, for example, going for a walk or a run.

Dietrich makes it clear, however, that creativity is unlikely to be just one of these modes on its own. The key to creative thinking (and this appears to hold true regardless of which model or vocabulary you might choose to use) seems to lie in *switching back-and-forth between these modes*. If we go back to the Jungian point of view, for example, encouraging you to make use of different types of conscious thinking, exploring the relationship between conscious and unconscious or directed and non-directed thinking can work to engage creative thought. Flipping between modes is what makes for a good creative mental space.

In the introduction we said that formats contained three paradoxes ("real but not real", "global but local" and "the same but different"), but it turns out that creativity itself requires paradoxical skills. That back-and-forth between directed, deliberate modes of information seeking purposeful, focused, intentionally curious *and* non-directed modes, spontaneous, being open to new experiences, daydreaming, where serendipity is key, whilst making use of the possibilities of physical motion to activate a flow mode. *All* of these modes may be necessary to helping you to find a possible idea. The fundamental to being creative (if we leave aside personality traits *per se*) is in a flexible approach, where you work to develop practices or habits that help to keep you moving back-and-forth between focus and daydreaming.

Being Creative?

As artist Philippa Stanton puts it in her book *Conscious Creativity*:

> Creativity is about discovering your own ways of working, your own unique practice, and growing the confidence needed to accept that. It's not about learning to create something like everyone else, it's about learning how to acknowledge the true value of what *you* do.
>
> (Stanton, 2018, p. 9)

Remember, creativity isn't an inborn trait that some people "just have" and some people "just don't". It is something you can get better at and develop your confidence in by getting to know your inner psychic ecosystem and valuing periods of less directed thinking. As another writer put it more succinctly 'creativity is in large part a decision – a set of attitudes towards life' (Sternberg, 2019, p. 100) and you can *decide* to resist the discomfort of boredom, to pay closer attention to where you are right now, and what is around you, resist the easy fix of the hyperstimulation of the screen and learn to value and enhance your own creative practice. Be focussed *and* a dreamer. This is not a waste of time. In fact, it is essential!

Exercise: Flipping Modes

We all have different strengths and weaknesses and ways of doing things, and the "self" is not a static thing that can be easily put into a box. It is more like an ecosystem which grows and changes over time, and to which you can attend to, or not, but which will continue to grow regardless. However, with a little care and attention, you can develop habits and attitudes that will improve your creativity.

Take a notebook and go to sit in your favourite place. It might be a busy café or under a quiet tree, in your bedroom or the middle of the town centre. It doesn't matter, though your choice of location might already start to tell you something about your habits and preferences. And whilst you can take notes on your phone or laptop, you might find the practice of using a notebook and a pen helps to keep you in the moment, and not distracted by a screen.

Set a timer for five minutes. In that time, your task is to note down some of the things you can see, hear, smell, touch, maybe even taste. Try to include how you perceive them through your senses. How many did you get? It's not a test, but practice in being present in your moment and surroundings and carrying out a focus-driven task.

Set the timer for another five minutes. Now try to capture any fleeting memories, intuitions, emotions, thoughts that may be attached to those things. By now, you might be thinking about one particular thing but allow your mind to wander. Does it remind you of that time when… Does it annoy you when… Is your favourite thing when… Did your dad always say… The best thing ever was… My dog is so funny… follow those little thoughts wherever they lead even into fantasy and "what if"…. what would it be like to… what if that were a giant or a tiny version… what if I could fly… what if that tree could talk… You might jot down a few things as they occur to you, but don't try and order things or tidy them up.

This activity should help you flit between the spontaneous/default mode, and a more focussed mode, whilst at the same time helping you to pay attention to your inner ecosystem. Try it over a few sessions, your notes will help you become aware of where your thoughts habitually take you. How easily do you slip from the "here and now" into a more spontaneous mode? Which is easier? Can you start to expand and explore the bit you find more difficult? Focussing on now, or slipping into daydream?

For creativity, understanding your own inner self better can be a good place to start and you can consider Jung's typology with regard to your conscious ways of functioning, even if it is only so far as the attitudes of introversion or extroversion. But you can also start to give attention to some of your unconscious ways of functioning too, perhaps through thinking about your dreams more, or through other active imagination activities, or arrange to have the time to let your mind wander and *valuing* those moments when your mind wanders. For some people staring out of a window works, for others, movement is essential such as going for a walk or a run, or even sitting on a bus or a train. Make time and space to deliberately flip between the different modes.

Some of these may be hard to bring into your workspace. Whilst we think your boss should let you go for a walk to enhance your creativity, they may not agree, but you can still do it on your commute, or you can do the senses exercise sitting at your desk or imagine yourself being in a place you know well and do it. Make these into habits that suit you and your current workplace. And maybe one day you'll find yourself in a place where you are allowed to go for a walk to enhance your thinking. Or you'll set up your own company around these practices. This is just the beginning.

Chapter 3 will take you through some of the models that were developed over the 20th century to help make creativity into a more deliberate process, before offering you our own model specific to TV formats. Keep your eye out for the switching between modes.

References

Beebe, J., 2017, *Energies and Patterns in Psychological Type: The reservoir of Consciousness*, Abingdon, Routledge.

Cotter, K., Christensen, A. & Silvia, P. 2019, Creativity's Role in Everyday Life, in J Kaufman & R Sternberg (eds), *Cambridge Handbook of Creativity*, Cambridge, Cambridge University press, pp. 640–651.

Dietrich, A., 2015, *How Creativity Happens in the Brain*, Basingstoke, Palgrave Macmillan.

Dietrich, A., 2019, Types of Creativity, *Psychonomic Bulletin & Review*, 26, pp. 1–12.

The Foundation of the Works of CG Jung, 2018, *The Art of C. G. Jung*, New York, W. W. Norton.

Glăveanu, V. & Kaufman, J. 2019, Creativity: A Historical Perspective, in J Kaufman & R Sternberg (eds), *Cambridge Handbook of Creativity*, Cambridge, Cambridge University Press, pp. 9–26.

Hillman, J., 1999, *The Myth of Analysis: Three Essays in Archetypal Psychology*, Evanston, Illinois, North Western University Press.

Jung, C.G., 1960, *Structure and Dynamics of the Psyche*, Hove, Routledge and Kegan Paul.

Jung, C.G., 1963, *Mysterium Coniunctionis: An Inquiry into the Separation and Synthesis of Psychic Opposites in Alchemy*, Hove, Routledge and Kegan Paul.

Kapoor, H. & Kaufman, J. 2022, Basic Concepts of Creativity, in S Russ, J Hoffman & J Kaufman (eds), *The Cambridge Handbook of Lifespan Development of Creativity*, Cambridge, Cambridge University Press, pp. 5–19.

Kaufman, J.C. & Beghetto, R.A., 2009, Beyond Big and Little: The Four C Model of Creativity, *Review of General Psychology*, 13, pp. 1–12.

Matthews, P. & Nalbantian, S. (eds), 2019, *Secrets of Creativity: What Neuroscience, the Arts, and Our Minds Reveal*, New York, Oxford University Press.

Parsons, T., 2017, *Cyberpsychology and the Brain: The Interaction of Neuroscience and Affective Computing*, Cambridge, Cambridge University Press.

Plucker, J., Makel, M. & Qian, M., 2019, Assessment of Creativity, in J Kaufman & R Sternberg (eds), *Cambridge Handbook of Creativity*, Cambridge, Cambridge University Press, pp. 44–68.

Samuels, A., Shorter, B. & Plaut, F., 1991, *A Critical Dictionary of Jungian Analysis*, London, Routledge.

Schaverien, J. (2005) Art, Dreams and Active Imagination: A Post-Jungian Approach to Transference and the Image. *Journal of Analytical Psychology*, 50, pp. 127–153.

Sharp, D., 1987, *Personality Types: Jung's Model of Typology*, Toronto, Inner City Books.

Stanton, P., 2018, *Conscious Creativity*, London, The Quarto Group.

Sternberg, R. 2019, Enhancing People's Creativity, in J Kaufman & R Sternberg (eds), *Cambridge Handbook of Creativity*, Cambridge, Cambridge University press, pp. 88–103.

Swan-Foster, N., 2020, C.G. Jung's Influence on Art Therapy and the Making of the Third, *Psychological Perspectives: A Quarterly Journal of Jungian Thought*, 63(1), pp. 67–94.

Vartanian, O. 2019, Neuroscience of Creativity, in J Kaufman & R Sternberg (eds), *Cambridge Handbook of Creativity*, Cambridge, Cambridge University press, pp. 148–172.

Wallas, G., 1926, *The Art of Thought*, London, Jonathan Cape.

3 Do Creative

In Chapter 2 we explored the inward-facing individual potential of your own psychology and how that can help you become aware of your own patterns of thinking. The helpful thing about Jung's model of the psyche is that it suggests we have access to many different styles of thinking, and that even if we find some easier than others, it's always worth the effort to work on those areas we're less naturally drawn to. We also suggested that the answer to the question, "where do ideas come from", is always ultimately *you*, but in this chapter, we'll see that this doesn't mean that they come out of thin air. Well, if you are extremely lucky, they might, but there is a lot you can do to help this process along and make the chances of success much, much higher.

You'll see that we draw on a range of sources for our approach to creating formats and we'll outline some of the background research first, before suggesting activities and practical tools to inspire and generate that first kernel of a format idea. Even if you *still* think you're not particularly creative, trying out some of these practices will help get the ball rolling.

Creativity as a Process: Some Background

One of the earliest attempts to codify the creative process (as opposed to listing creative personality traits) was a book published in 1926, called *The Art of Thought*, where Graham Wallas laid out four stages of the creative process, based on his own observations and the accounts of various artists and inventors (Wallas, 1926). (There is a fifth-stage "intimation" between incubation and illumination which indicates a solution is close, but most modern accounts of Wallas's model leave this out, as we do here.) Wallas was the first to capture not just the "aha!" moment but what comes before *and* after it. Whilst the model has proved somewhat contentious over the years, with critics suggesting it is too simplistic, it can still be a surprisingly useful place to start. In fact, many subsequent and more complex approaches to creativity can be quite easily mapped onto Wallas's four stages, which also, intriguingly, can be associated with the neuroscience proposals of the deliberate and spontaneous modes of creative thinking and Jung's directed and non-directed styles of thinking.

DOI: 10.4324/9781003050650-3

Briefly, the stages are:

- Preparation – getting ready, pump priming, deciding what the question or task is.
- Incubation – although it might seem that nothing is happening, nevertheless, the mind keeps working even whilst doing other things.
- Illumination – the "aha!" moment, the "here's an idea" moment (the thing people often think of as *the* creative moment).
- Verification – where the idea is tested, "is it fit for purpose?", maybe it is expanded upon, and perhaps even implemented.

Wallas's four stages were already breaking down the assumption that ideas strike from nowhere, in fact quite the opposite. His "preparation" stage is vital. It sounds obvious, but you have to know that you're looking for something to know when you've found it, but he also leaves room for spontaneous discovery and exploration in the "incubation" phase.

Creativity research received a major injection of energy in the mid-20th century when JP Guilford (1897–1987) made a speech at the American Psychological Association in 1950. This speech is often seen as a turning point for creativity research and Guildford's address certainly did a great deal to focus some serious research into creativity, though he did not, as it were, "invent" it then and there. He noted in later years that he had been able to articulate 'an undercurrent of need felt for increased creative performance and a desire to know more about the nature of creativity itself' (Guilford, 1958a, p. 142). It was the right speech at the right time. Guilford's own research led him to establish the Structure of Intellect model, which recognised different dimensions to intelligence (see Guilford, 1956, 1967), an idea which became particularly influential in education (see Meeker, 1969).

The Structure of Intellect model explored three major areas of thinking factors, as he called them: cognition, production and evaluation. He split the production factor – so called because they produce some end result – into two areas, which he called convergent production – moving towards one conclusion or answer – and divergent production where 'there is much searching or going off in various directions' (Guilford, 1956, p. 274). In a later paper he acknowledged that it was 'in the divergent-thinking category that we find the abilities most pertinent to creative thinking' (Guilford, 1958b, p. 14). The concept of divergent thinking (as it came to be called) consisted of fluency, flexibility, originality and elaboration, and has been very influential in creativity studies, in many cases standing in as a proxy for creativity itself. This was because Guilford was able to construct reliable and repeatable tests for these factors that made them useful for other disciplines. However, Guildford himself was more cautious making clear 'It cannot be truthfully said that only divergent-thinking abilities contribute to creative production, for other categories of intellectual resources play their parts' (Guilford, 1958b, p. 14).

There are two particular points that make Guilford's work of continuing interest to us. Firstly, he recognised the opening-up (divergent thinking) and closing-down (convergent thinking) aspects of the creative process that we might associate with the spontaneous mode and the deliberate mode that we discussed in Chapter 2, and you might see this push–pull reflected in our *Prepare* and *Play* sections below. The second point is that the work around divergent thinking and its modes of fluency and flexibility in particular have become an almost standard part of ideas generation. Fluency relates to the number of ideas, whilst flexibility denotes freedom from rigidity, which we might today refer to as "thinking outside the box". Again, you will recognise some of this in other parts of the book.

In his 1958 article "Can Creativity be Developed", Guilford directly named Alex Osborn (1888–1966) of the advertising firm Batton, Barton, Durstine and Osborn in making use of his "brain-storming session" 'for the generation of new ideas for use in advertising' (Guilford, 1958b, p. 16). However, the connection went both ways, and the Preface to Osborn's book called *Applied Imagination* and published in 1953, made direct reference to Guilford's research (and the book makes use of Wallas's ideas too). The contribution that Osborn is remembered for today was in recognising that 'Properly organised and run, a group can be creatively productive to an extraordinary degree' (Osborn, 1953, p. 297). He had begun using group-thinking sessions (as they were originally called) as early as 1939, but the participants themselves dubbed it "brainstorming" meaning 'using the brain to storm a creative problem – and to do so in *commando* fashion, with each stormer audaciously attacking the same objective' (Osborn, 1953, p. 297). Osborn made use of the ideas about fluency and quantity but set them to work in a group setting. Osborn went on to found the Creative Education Foundation, and, with Sidney J Parnes, an academic at Buffalo State College, New York, developed the Creative Problem-Solving Process, which is still being taught by the Foundation today.

The 1960s saw further work on the question of creativity, with Edward de Bono (1933–2021), making perhaps one of the most popularly known contributions. de Bono was a doctor, philosopher and psychologist who introduced the idea of lateral thinking. This wasn't initially about creativity as such but formed part of the programme for the CoRT (Cognitive Research Trust) which aimed to create free thinking students. This model emphasised a number of things such as a breadth of interests, and ways to systematise thinking and assess information (see Sternberg, 2019), but the concept of lateral thinking is the one that is most relevant to our focus on creativity.

Whilst critical thinking is primarily concerned with judging the true value of statements and seeking errors (which we might relate back to Guilford's convergent thinking or Jung's directed thinking), 'With lateral thinking we move "sideways" to try different perceptions, different concepts, different points of entry' (de Bono, 1992, p. 53). Though de Bono was also at pains to point out that divergent thinking is a *part* of lateral thinking and not a direct equivalent (de Bono, 1992, p. 55). In de Bono's model, the brain is predisposed to making patterns out of perceptions, such as "cause and effect", and so to go against the grain, to cut across patterns, is what is essential to see new ideas. As he observed, 'In our thinking we find ourselves looking harder and harder in the same direction because that is where our expertise and intellectual investment has been. It becomes difficult to move away in a fresh direction' (de Bono, 1991, p. 243). In fact, de Bono often used the analogy of a river valley to explain the problem. 'There are the main tracks of perception… which, like river valleys, collect all information in the neighbourhood. Everything flows into the existing "rivers"' (de Bono, 1992, p. 39). The important element that de Bono brings to our attention is the importance of not getting too stuck in our ways and allowing our brains to mould everything into the same old patterns. We have to stay curious and be open to new experiences and ways of doing things in order to be truly creative.

This is a very short introduction to some of the underpinning ideas that form the process we outline below, but let's explore these insights in a practical way and take you through some places to start as well as offering some tips and advice. We summarise this part of the Development Circle as *Prepare, Play, Participate, Identify the Purpose* and *Get Picky*.

Prepare

As so much of the research makes clear, you have to start by realising that there is a task in hand and that there is something to be done. In Chapter 2 we mentioned the deliberate mode, which might involve information seeking and setting parameters. What is it you need to do? Come up with an idea for a format? Ok, but that's a big ask to arrive out of nowhere. So, if it seems just too big and intimidating, why not break it down into some smaller tasks? Richard McKerrow, co-creator with Anna Beattie of *The Great British Bake Off* (Love Productions, 2010–present), observed 'people say, how did you come up with *Bake Off*. There was no one moment… There are [only] moments when there's a bit more of a lightbulb'. So, rather than being intimidated about immediately finding *the* idea, begin instead by seeking out five "starting points". These might include a commissioning brief you have been asked to work towards, your own passion or topic, memories, observations, something you saw in the news, something you saw in the street, perhaps even something you noticed or imagined when you did the exercise in the previous chapter? But let's break that down even further into places to start looking for inspiration for your starting points.

Commissioning briefs are an important starting point, especially if you are working in a development team where discussions will often start with new intelligence on what a channel or commissioner wants. In terms of formats, there are rarely commissioning briefs specifically on format needs, though many commissioners will tell you that formats are highly sought after due to their repeatability and returnability making them a cost-effective, reliable, stalwart in any schedule, with possibilities for additional profit from IP sales and distribution deals, brand equity and talent development. So, a good starting place is to get into the habit of reading commissioning briefs, often found on Broadcaster and platform websites, and note down what they are after, what are the key words and also their production budgets (programme tariffs). Even if you are not already working in a production team, most of this sort of information is available online, especially for the public service broadcasting channels in the UK. The following was taken from BBC1's Entertainment brief when this book went to press; they were looking for 'new territories, perfect talent, celebrity driven, reinvent the competitive shape, broad appeal' (BBC, n.d.).

However, commissioners' needs can change at the drop of a hat and many of the developers we spoke to argue that a good idea will be commissioned regardless of the brief, especially now that there are so many buyers. As Stephen Lambert noted 'There's more opportunity because there are more buyers', before going on to explain,

> in the past we would often go to one of the three UK buyers (Channel 4, BBC and ITV) with the seed of an idea and kind of create the show with them, particularly with Channel 4. Once that dialogue had started, there was a clear understanding one didn't pitch that idea to any other buyer. Now, there are so many different buyers with all the SVODs and US networks, and the selling process has changed. We need to be much clearer about the idea and work it out in great detail before we pitch it, but once we get to that point, we pitch that developed idea to all suitable buyers and see who wants to make the best deal.

Knowing what commissioners are looking for can be an excellent place to start, but at the same time, a "good idea is a good idea" and need not be reliant on current commissioning calls. So, if good ideas will find a commissioning home regardless, where else can we look for starting points? Of course, the internet is full of, well, everything! But it can be a bit much to explore with the added difficulty that algorithms might be keeping you in a bubble of things that you've previously shown an interest in. Social media is also helpful, but topics tend to flare up and die down quickly, which isn't much good from a production point of view. However, there are other avenues, and if you are a keen inhabitant of the online world, stepping out of that routine might be your very first challenge in changing your habits (or indeed vice versa).

A first suggestion is that you could go looking for starting points in newspapers. In 2004, Stephen Lambert explained the source of the idea for *Wife Swap* (RDF Media, 2003–2009, 2017):

> We were looking at things like an article in the *Daily Mail* about how a nurse on £15,000 lived, compared with a barrister on £200,000. What about them swapping lives, then what about a wife swap? … no, we couldn't do it. Then we thought hang on, there are separate bedrooms. We embarked on it.
>
> (Brown, 2004)

Magazines can also offer valuable starting points. It is certainly true that the print format has been declining, but this has affected newspaper sales far more than the magazine sector and there is a wonderful array of magazine titles on offer. From mainstream classics like *Vogue* (Condé Nast) through to the more niche offerings such as *PLY* (an independently published magazine for spinners, as in wool and spinning wheels) and *Modern Railways* (Key Publishing), a magazine can offer an amazing window into another world in a far more contained way than a website might do, and the small ads contain a wealth of information about wants and needs in that world.

The dating show now known as *Love in the Countryside* (Boundless Productions, 2018), originally came from an article in *Country Living* magazine (Hearst Magazines UK). Following a campaigning "lonely hearts" feature back in 1997, the *Country Living* office was inundated with mail from country-dwelling singles looking for love. In those early days, the team acted as matchmakers by passing on letters between those who wrote in, but then it became a TV series (as explained on www.farmerwantsawife.co.uk, n.d.). In fact, the show was originally known as *Farmer Wants a Wife* (Thames Television, 2001/Fremantle Media 2009), and premiered in the UK in 2001, but then travelled around the world. The Australian version has at least 11 series.

With the rise of open access publishing, academic journals are also an easily available resource, chock full of fresh insights and new ideas, and Channel 4 show *Naked Beach* (Barefaced TV, 2019) was developed from research carried out by a social psychologist at Goldsmiths University of London. Many open-access journals are also available online.

However, these starting points might also come from your own life and experience. Ana de Moraes, creator of *First Dates* (Twenty Twenty/Warner Bros. Television Productions UK 2013–present) said, 'Ideas tend to come from the real world in some shape or form so [they are] things that happen and that people will be able to relate to'. Richard McKerrow said

> for me where I look back and figure where [ideas] came from, they come from you, they come from what's happening in your life personally so if I'm with a development person I say well what's happening with you? It comes from … the immediate world around you.

Nell Butler, now Joint CEO of Riverdog Productions, explained how the starting point for *Come Dine with Me* (ITV Studios, 2005–present) came from her own experience of what she called 'my most disastrous dinner party'.

> They [the guests] arrived early, I was cooking couscous for the first time, and I was totally out of my depth. After the guests left at the end of the evening and my husband sank into a chair, he said "well, I'd give that a three" and we really laughed.

But it did set her thinking about the idea of "competitive entertaining" and the show developed from there.

However, even at this stage of seeking these starting points, you will want to keep an eye on habits forming. If you do the same thing every day with the same people, you will come up with the same ideas. Sitting in a production meeting where you all read the same articles or newspapers online will lead to the same ideas. Be alert to opportunities to challenge yourself. Go somewhere different. Walk around a neighbourhood you've never been to. Invite people to your production meetings. Stay open to what you see. If you are exploring a topic, list your assumptions about it and then challenge them one by one. Be aware you may have preconceptions and biases and find ways to challenge them. Enlist your senses – go to the place where they happen and *really* look at the detail – what do people do when they arrive, what do they get excited by, how does it feel?

So, pay attention to what is around you, but then take the time to record your observations. You never know when that "starting point" will turn into *the* big idea. Remember wondering if that tree could talk in Chapter 2? Maybe imagining what that tree would tell you is the starting point for a factual history format about place.

Play

Remember that it is important to stay flexible and move back and forth between deliberate parameter setting and spontaneity. Don't get stuck in one or the other. Don't, as Edward de Bono might have put it, "get stuck in your riverbed"! Once you have collected your starting points, it is important to start playing with the ideas. As Alex Osborn said, 'Freewheeling is welcomed!' (Osborn, 1953, p. 300).

One suggestion, building on divergent thinking, is to use one of the starting points to generate a lot of ideas about and around that topic. As many as you can come up with. They don't have to be amazing or more than tangentially relevant. Just go for it. Quantity can come before quality. This is sometimes called a "brain dump" where you get everything out of your head and onto the page. Find five, then another five and another five and *then* maybe you start to reach the really interesting stuff, the new stuff. The key premise is not to accept the first idea that pops into your head. By generating many options and keeping ideas topline, with sparse production detail, you are more likely to exhaust the obvious ideas and find new, original thinking.

Another possibility to shake things up is to work with forced connections in a "combine-connect-challenge" exercise. When creating *Take a Hike* (Cardiff Productions, 2021–present) for S4C in Wales, nationally for BBC2 and now selling internationally, Narinder Minhas and the team made the connection between a popular territory of "walking" and a factual entertainment approach. This created a new topline idea where five hikers compete to lead the best walk, judged on the route, picnic, views and fun. Other tools used by Narinder to make forced connections include (to paraphrase) – what if …we mixed together Topic X, with a Y approach, and add a colour Z; adding a dominant "flavour" or emotion to a topic or idea. What if… we make audiences cry, laugh, think or get angry? What if we use song titles as starting points? Why not look at the singles charts and try turning the Top Ten tracks into shows? In Chapter 4 we suggest some types of formats. What if you mix up one type of format with an unusual topic? Or in Chapter 7 we talk about casting – can you find unusual participants for a familiar idea? Or go large? What if we had a hundred judges instead of three as was the case in the singing format *All Together Now* (Remarkable Television/ Banijay, 2018). Mix and match the potential elements.

In this phase be silly, put ridiculous things together, try for opposites, take it to the next level. What if you had an enormous budget? What if you had very little budget? What if you really hate that topic, or really can't stand that type of show, well, what would need to happen to make you watch it? What version of it would you find irresistible? If you already love that topic or type of show, what is the *one* bit that you really love? What happens if you focus on that to the exclusion of all else? Be playful, turn things on their head, mix it up and keep it moving. de Bono talks about movement, saying 'The general sense of "movement" means the willingness to move forward in a positive exploring way rather than stopping to judge whether something is right or wrong' (de Bono, 1992, p. 153). Great advice!

Participate

We have been a little vague up until now about whether you might be working solo or with others, but the truth is it will almost certainly be a bit of both. Chapter 8 covers the people aspect in more detail but collaborating with others is a key skill. As Jonathan Meenagh put it, 'a lot of these things are huge collaborations with lots of different people, with different ideas and there's no one single person who had the monopoly on the vision' whilst Narinder Minhas went a bit further saying,

> you can't do this on your own. It's really, really hard. And I want to stress that. You've got to have a development team that has a range of skills. You've got to have people who are also diverse in different ways, that actually think in a different way.

They aren't alone. Every executive producer, development executive or chief creative officer will tell you that it is the bringing together of different thinking and development that makes great ideas happen. From development teams, to sharing with your family, to working with commissioners, ideas thrive on diversity of voices. We will cover this further in Chapter 8, Drive it, where we consider creating an "Ideas Team" to support and drive your thinking.

Osborn formulated the brainstorming technique in the 1950s and although it has been in and out of fashion over the years, there is no doubt that it remains a useful tool, not only in generating ideas but in helping you to play with them, tossing them about and knocking the corners off. The ability to defend and challenge ideas with others is vital. There really is no better way of testing the strength of an idea and finding angles you might have missed, and in fact moving from "mini-c" to "little-c" creativity and then onto "Pro-C" creativity requires you to not only generate ideas, but to share them and test them with other people (see Kapoor & Kaufman, 2022).

There are a great many resources available online to help run a productive brainstorming session and we don't want to reiterate them all here, but the important thing is to set clear parameters in terms of the task, such as a time limit and perhaps even assigning a scribe to take notes, as well as explicitly articulating and modelling the expected conduct of participants, such as a call to be generous and build on each other's ideas. An open atmosphere, making others feel safe, comfortable and free from fear of failure is essential. Ana de Moraes of MultiStory Media, creator of *First Dates*, describes this creative space as safe, a chance for everyone to get stuck in, equal and inclusive, with playful starting points and guessing games. She said,

> It's about being playful… and there are a lot of bad ideas, but in the room let them come up and you talk about it, and you move things on gently if people start getting excited about an idea that you don't think is good as it doesn't fit the brief… In the room it needs to be fun, and it needs to be safe. People might feel like they're going to make a mistake but there is no such thing as a mistake in a brainstorm.

At the same time, a collective brainstorming session is of little use if it descends into blandness and everyone agreeing on the most nondescript idea. As Kate Phillips, the BBC's Entertainment Controller put it, she'd always rather have "a show that people reacted strongly to, one way or the other" than one that invoked indifference.

Participating in collective ideas generation can require a good level of emotional awareness, a complex blend of willingness to speak up with an idea, but also a willingness to listen to others; being ready to defend and challenge and being aware of your own ruts, without getting defensive or confrontational; and knowing when to let things go (to be saved for another day perhaps) or when to stick to your guns. You may find it helpful to go back over Chapter 2 to explore your inner ecosystem one more time. In Chapter 8, we will explore these people skills in more depth, with techniques to help you believe in your ideas and get others to believe in them too.

Identify the Purpose – the Big TEASER

Once you've played around with your starting points and perhaps had a chance to try them with other people, maybe it feels like you are onto something! You have the kernel of an idea to focus on. The next step is to find the hook, to find the heart of the idea, its purpose, by simplifying your topic into one simple engaging question or insight. Nell Butler, creator of *Come Dine with Me* suggested that

> You …have to have that absolute one-liner guiding principle that really means that people get and love the heart of the format. The good formats you recognise. It's the one where they have to eat disgusting creepy crawlies,

the one where he says "You're fired!" *Come Dine with Me* is the one where they score dinner parties in the back of a taxi.

So, can you sum up your idea easily? Does it still take quite a long time to explain? How do you cut to the chase? It might be necessary to bring things back to earth a little. What might be possible?

We suggest you find the heart of your idea by working through the TEASER process below. TEASER literally helps *tease out ideas* by quickly discovering new questions or hooks for ideas. It might seem like we're going over some familiar territory but TEASER allows you to dig deeper, to turn your thinking, your starting points, into hooks or jumping-off sites for ideas that are more TV focused and can relate back to a commissioner brief.

TE: *Topics or Trends into Emotions*

As we've suggested, clues for format hooks are all around us. We are constantly exposed to news stories, reports, statistics and facts, information about new consumer behaviours and attitudes, social movements, economic, political and technological trends; this technique turns any interesting fact or statistic into a hook for ideas! A trend or new topic may answer the BBC1 commissioning brief for new territory, but it is only when you find the emotions inherent in the idea that it really comes to life. Caroline Roseman, Director of Development at Fulwell 73 Productions, explained that she asks her producers to look around statistics. She said,

> Statistics are a great starting point for ideas. Audiences want authenticity so to have a real-world starting point provides an instant connection between the idea you're developing and the audiences you're trying to reach. We often include statistics when we're playing "format cocktail" – a brainstorming mechanic a lot of development teams use. For example, you might have a box full of different statistics on pieces of paper, a box full of sitcom plots on pieces of paper and like a lucky dip you take one from each box and see if the two you picked out at random can inspire an idea.

Notice how quickly she introduces something as seemingly logical/rational as sets of statistics and then finds a way to play with them! In a 2013 interview, Peter Bazalgette explained how, although gardening had always been popular on television, 'we saw some research which informed us that young people were treating their gardens like they were treating their interiors. They weren't willing to plant some seeds and wait six months and learn how to garden. People wanted instant makeovers of gardens' (Bazalgette, 2013), and the result was *Ground Force* (Endemol, 1997–2005), a garden makeover show, which ran for 12 series. Bazalgette took the statistics of what was happening but crucially found the emotional core of *why* it was happening.

So, these are the questions to ask:

a   **What have you noticed that's interesting?** In addition to the earlier suggestions, one way to start is by thinking about what audience you are trying to appeal to? A quick internet search gives you access to insights and reports about every generation; what they are buying, what they are reading and what matters to them, and spending some time with this audience will unearth what matters to them, what are their fears, hopes and dreams; this is rich territory for new ideas. What are the topics and trends?
b   **Why is this important?** By itself an observation is not a format idea. It is with the use of the simple question, "why is this important?", that we begin to define new hooks for ideas. It is important to the audience to buy fully grown plants because "they want an instant garden, they can't be bothered to get their hands dirty planting seeds, they do not have time to tend to their plants, they have the money to buy a fully grown plant". These are all answers to the question, why is this important, and are often the starting points for new ideas. Where is the emotional need?
c   **How can we turn these into a simple, salient question (to hook audiences)?** For example, How can we show how to get an instant garden?
d   **What's the new idea?** As discussed, you can then take the question and go for a quantity of topline ideas; remember that at this stage you are not looking to work up an idea, to develop the story or format. Instead think about what is new; what is fresh; what is different and what is the want or need. Peter Bazalgette's insight about a garden centre trend for buying fully grown plants led in time to *Ground Force* which was first broadcast in 1997 on BBC2 but was so successful that the series moved to BBC1 for the second series. The series was credited with helping the increase in sales of garden decking in the late 1990s and early 2000s due to its use during the series. Retailer B&Q had sales rise from £5,000 in 1997 to £16 million in 2001 (Francis, 2001). At its peak, the series attracted 12 million viewers. *Ground Force America* on BBC America first aired in 2003 and was its first original Production. But Bazalgette recognised that desire for a finished garden right now.

A: Access

Another way to hone your starting points is to consider if you might cast a light into the shadows of life, meaning give the audience access to something they don't normally get to see. *One Born Every Minute* (Dragonfly/Endemol Shine UK, 2010–2018) gives us an up-close view of childbirth. *Naked Attraction* (Studio Lambert, 2016–present) starts where a good date might end! Less sensationally, although just as effectively, for Ana de Moraes and her team it was looking at the unseen side of dating on TV which led to *First Dates*. de Moraes describes how the team realised that past dating shows were "artificial" representations of reality, as you were unlikely to go on a "jet skiing holiday on your first date together!" When they were asked to film a pilot for Channel 4 on the real side of dating in a rather smart, real restaurant, they discovered that rather than seeking the car crash TV of mismatched couples, it was the matched couples which led to the mesmerising watch of first love. Does your idea or *could* your idea offer an inside view, a behind-the-scenes view or even a never-seen-before view of your topic? Again, finding something that is hidden is just the first step, asking *why* this is hidden, the purpose, will deliver jumping-off points for ideas; for *One Born Every Minute*, the answer might be that childbirth is hidden because it is an intimate, private moment, so "How could we be a fly-on-the-wall" of a maternity unit?

S: *Success*

Another lucrative avenue for ideas is to "steal success" from shows, brands, books, talent or even platforms by understanding why these are successful, what appeals to their audience, what keeps them watching? Out and out originality isn't always everything, you can find new format ideas from what already works! Of course, we don't mean simply replicating a pre-existing idea (of course not!), but when Jonathan Meenagh was asked about the development of the successful format, *Hunted* (Shine TV/Banijay, 2015–present), he explained it was inspired by his experience on *The Island with Bear Grylls* (Shine TV/Banijay, 2014–present) now in its seventh series. *The Island* featured different groups of people surviving on a remote, uninhabited Island with only basic tools and training, whilst *Hunted* is a kind of thriller competition where ordinary people go on the run from a team of expert hunters. However, he said,

> creating a lineage of TV success... always starts with one piece of innovation which has either been tested, which has been thought through well and then executed well or executed well enough... and then you can do it again and build on it.

Core to the approach to *The Island* was a search for authenticity and key to that was the decision to put the film crew on the island 'to live and work in the same conditions as the individuals who are on the programme and to feature on the programme, to turn the cameras round on themselves'. They also found their hook when Jay Hunt, Creative Officer for Channel 4 at the time, realised that 'everything in this show has to be life or death and every scene has to be life or death', which is also a great illustration of how important contributions can come from all sorts of directions. *The Island* wasn't about in-fighting or personal dramas, it was about survival and the hook was "Could you survive on a desert island?" Meenagh continued,

> All of the things that we learned from [*The Island*] went in to create *Hunted*, where again there was a very clear question at the heart of that "could you go on the run" and... how do we make that as authentic as possible... and at the beginning of the *Hunted* development, we started with an embedded crew.

So, although the two shows are very different, recognising the right elements – the search for authenticity and the filming device of an embedded crew – helped one develop the other.

The important thing here is to develop your understanding of how shows work (or not). If there are shows you admire, why? *Why* do they work? What can you learn from them? You could go back to your notes from the Chapter 1. How can you combine the successful elements (topic, filming device, production style, casting and so on) with your fresh idea? And you might want to come back to this question yet again after reading the chapters on form, design and characters. Remember development rarely goes in one straight line.

E: *Extremes*

Every now and then there is an opportunity to work with a "challenger" channel, brand or commissioner; these are channels, platforms or even talent that are looking to challenge audience perceptions or break completely new ground. This is rich territory that can shed light on the best of life and the worst, extreme situations, human reactions and behaviours; it also allows us to question our own expectations and reactions to topics, genres and formats, turning them on their heads. So, how can you push your idea to the limits? If you had the option to *really* go for it, where would you take the idea? In terms of a travel format, Studio Lambert created *Race Across the World* (Studio Lambert, 2019–present) where pairs race to reach a distant destination by any method except plane, and the first series started in London and finished in Singapore. However, an E4 commission for production company Avalon brought together survival with a travel competition in *Naked, Alone and Racing to Get Home* the premise of which the title explains rather well (Broadcast, 2022).

When Caroline Roseman and the team at Whizz Kid Entertainment came up with *Ex on the Beach* (2014–present), it was built on:

> the feeling you get when you walk into a supermarket, and you haven't brushed your hair or done your make-up and then you see your ex walking towards you. Everyone understands just how gut-wrenching that would be. There's something about exes that inspires a visceral reaction in everyone. To come face-to-face with the person who broke your heart or whose heart you broke, who knows you inside and out. It always stirs emotion. So, to go on a dating show with the promise of finding love and then find that your exes are coming – it's like a horror movie in paradise and that's the tone we tried to brand that format with.

It's the extreme nightmare version of a holiday romance!

R: *Real Life*

As we suggested earlier, real life is often a great inspiration for ideas, such as Nell Butler's disastrous dinner party. Inspiration can take many forms, but it is often a heightened depiction of real-life events. When Gerard Costello took up executive producing *Location, Location, Location* (IWC Media, 2000–present), he was told that the inspiration from the idea came from how one-sided the property market was for everyday house buyers:

> As I understand it… what *Location, Location, Location* arose from was the awareness of a need that wasn't being satisfied in the real world. Buying a house is one of the most difficult things you will ever do, one of the most stressful things you will ever do, most likely the biggest purchase you'll ever make and yet the realisation was that nobody was on your side when you wanted to do it. The British property market was on the side of selling the house. What happened in the real word was that, at the very high end of property buying, you had people who were like estate agents for the buyer. They were property finders for people at the more exclusive end of the market. This is something that TV formats can do very well; democratise a service that actually exists. It takes it and puts it into the grasp of more people.

Location, Location, Location gives the participants and the audience access to property finders without paying for it!

Exercise: Practice Makes Perfect

If you are still not sure, why not practice with some shows you know well. An internet search might reveal what the original starting point or insight for the show is, especially if it is one of the well-established formats. Then, using the TEASER Grid, can you figure out the emotional hook? Hooks are what get people to want to watch your TV format and they are at the heart of every great TV format, and the more you practice with pre-existing shows, the more you will be able to discern the possibilities in your own starting points.

Table 3.1 summarises the TEASER questions so you can refer to them quickly.

Get Picky

The final challenge at this stage is to start narrowing things down again. So, one of the challenges of divergent thinking, where you generate many ideas or options, is that you will need to select the best ideas to go into the next stage of development. This selection stage correlates with Wallas's Verification stage of the process or Guilford's convergent thinking, because whilst there is a phase where it is important to open up and play with ideas in an uncritical way, there is also a time to close down and focus on what is required. Time to get picky!

The TEASER Grid might have already helped you focus in on the purpose or heart of one of your ideas, but these four key factors below will be useful to evaluating ideas through your own gut preferences but also keeping in mind your potential commissioner's:

Table 3.1 TEASER Grid

TEASER Grid

	T – E	A	S	E	R
	Topical – Emotion	Access	Success	Extremes	Real Life
Used for	New topics or audiences	New topics or genres	New platforms for audiences New audiences on platforms	New genre or format revolutions	New topics, genres, audiences
Description	Turns audience behaviours, topics and trends into emotional needs	Identifies unexplored interest in universal themes and debunks common misconceptions	Translates the formulae for successful content into audience appeal	Takes a fresh look at well-known topics, themes, genres and formats	Explores life in new ways, from making it more real to making it magical reality
Key questions	1 What's interesting? 2 Why is this important? 3 How can we turn this into a simple, salient hook? 4 What are the format ideas?	1 What's a hidden universal or what's missing on TV? 2 Why is this hidden? 3 How can we turn this into a simple, salient hook? 4 What are the format ideas?	1 What show, brand, strand, platform, etc. is successful? 2 Why is it successful? 3 How can we turn this into a simple, salient hook? 4 What are the format ideas?	1 What's the worst or best that could happen when…? 2 Why? 3 How can we turn this into a simple, salient hook? 4 What are the format ideas?	1 What have you noticed? 2 Why is it interesting? 3 How can we turn this into a simple, salient hook? 4 What are the format ideas?
Example hooks	How can we show how to get an instant garden?	How can we match couples for love at first sight?	How can we show who will survive… being hunted?	How can we show "the ex" showing up on holiday?	How can we give buyers someone that's on their side?
Formats	Ground Force (Endemol, 1997–2005)	First Dates (Twenty Twenty/Warner Bros. Television Productions UK, 2013–present)	Hunted (Shine TV/Banijay, 2015–present)	Ex on the Beach (Whizz Kid Entertainment, 2014–present)	Location, Location, Location (IWC Media/Banijay, 2004–present)

- *Imagination* – is this idea imaginative, different, unique? It is much more appealing to work on an idea that will stretch you, your audience and clients. Although sometimes considering the relative "freshness" of an idea is more helpful than out and out originality. Television is often an industry of incremental innovation than one of lightning strikes of originality, but, then again, not always.
- *Interest* – is this idea interesting to you? If *you* like the idea, then it is more likely that you will develop it to make it interesting to others. If you *don't* find it interesting, why do you assume others will? Be tough, be picky.
- *Influence* – is this an idea you have influence over? It is important to consider whether you have expertise or can convince others to make it for you.
- *Immediacy* – is this idea of the moment? If an idea feels like it is right for now, that it has an urgency to be heard, then it is more likely to succeed.

In this chapter we have considered a creative process for ideas generation. We have asked you to *Prepare, Play, Participate, Identify the Purpose* and then *Get Picky*. We have suggested places to begin looking for those all-important "starting points", which might become ideas strong enough to withstand the knockabout playful phase where you are likely to be working with others. Use any number of areas from the TEASER Grid to turn "Trends into Emotions, Access, Success, Extremes and Real Life" into question hooks and to find the emotional core or purpose of the idea. This central core is going to be vital as you start working through the next chapters. In the cut and thrust of development it can be easy to lose that original insight and hook, so keep it handy. It is your north star and your guiding light. It is at the heart of why your audience will want to watch the show and keep coming back for more.

Good formats have been a success for television because they often tap into something that an audience didn't even know it wanted. Whether it is drawing on a topical issue or a trend, or delivering to an audience's deeper emotional needs, the essence of a format relies on the simplicity of something we can all recognise, that has meaning or purpose, and winning formats tend to answer these universal needs on either a practical or an emotional level. For example, *Location, Location, Location* helps us buy a home; *Hunted* asks if we could survive going on the run and *First Dates* wonders whether love really is at first sight! Luckily for us, this universality means that we can all come up with a format idea.

In the next few chapters, we will explore how your topline ideas – these are just one-liner descriptions of your ideas, with their hooks – can be constructed and built into successful formats through their different structures, worlds, story arcs, cast and design, whilst always staying true to an exciting and enticing hook to draw the audience into your world.

References

Bazalgette, P., 2013, Interviewed by A. Coates for How Did They Do It, 2 July, Retrieved May 2, 2022, from https://howdidtheydoit.net/creative/sir-peter-bazalgette-television-entrepreneur/

BBC, no date, Popular Factual and Factual Entertainment, *bbc.co.uk*. Retrieved April 24, 2022, from www.bbc.co.uk/commissioning/factual-entertainment

Broadcast, 2022, Naked, Alone and Racing to Get Home Secures Series Commission, Retrieved May 2, 2022, from www.broadcastnow.co.uk/channel-4/naked-alone-and-racing-to-get-home-secures-series-commission/5169065.article

Brown, M., 2004, Swapping Success, *The Guardian*, Retrieved May 2, 2022, from www.theguardian.com/media/2004/oct/04/mondaymediasection.broadcasting.

de Bono, E., 1991, *I Am Right, You Are Wrong: From This to the New Renaissance: From Rock Logic to Water Logic*, London, Penguin Books.

de Bono, E., 1992, *Serious Creativity: Using the Power of Lateral Thinking to Create New Ideas*, London, HarperCollins Publisher.

Farmer Wants a Wife, no date, Retrieved May 2, 2022, from www.farmerwantsawife.co.uk/s/

Francis, C., 2001, Insurance: The Rise of the Green-Fingered Criminal Your Home May Be a Castle, but What about the Garden?, *The Independent*, April 15.

Guilford, J.P., 1956, The Structure of Intellect. *Psychological Bulletin*, 53(4), pp. 267–293.

Guilford, J.P., 1958a, Traits of Creativity, in H Anderson (ed), *Creativity and Its Cultivation: Addresses Presented at the Inter-disciplinary Symposia on Creativity*, New York, Harper & Row, pp. 142–161.

Guilford, J.P.,1958b, Can Creativity Be Developed? *Art Education*, 11(6), pp. 3–18.

Guilford, J.P.,1967, *The Nature of Human Intelligence*, New York, McGraw-Hill.

Kapoor, H. & Kaufman, J., 2022, Basic Concepts of Creativity, in S Russ, J Hoffman & J Kaufman (eds), *The Cambridge Handbook of Lifespan Development of Creativity*, Cambridge, Cambridge University Press, pp. 5–19.

Meeker, M.N.,1969, *The Structure of Intellect: Its Interpretation and Uses*, Columbus: Merrill.

Osborn, A.F., 1953, *Applied Imagination: Principles and Procedures of Creative Thinking*, New York, Charles Scribner's Sons.

Sternberg, R., 2019, Enhancing People's Creativity, in J Kaufman & R Sternberg (eds), *Cambridge Handbook of Creativity*, Cambridge, Cambridge University Press, pp. 88–103.

Wallas, G., 1926, *The Art of Thought*, London, Jonathan Cape.

4 Shape It

Chapters 2 and 3 explored how to be more creative and how to start unlocking your own creative process. The TEASER Grid gave you a set of questions to find the core of your idea, so by now you might have something intriguing starting to form, but even if you don't, keep reading. We're about to take you through the next stages of the Development Circle. Remember that although we keep going forward in the book, you can always go backwards to check or change previous ideas as you explore new elements of your format. It's important to keep asking questions throughout. Formats are not bashed out in a week. These processes can take months as you tighten, discard and change elements. It may feel repetitive at times, but each layer will bring out something new.

Now you have the first glimmer of an idea; let's look at how to turn it into a format. In the next four chapters we'll take you through what to look for when designing a format as you move from a hook and topline idea into a workable format. Much of this process comes from storytelling because, as we said in the introduction, a format is really a guarantee of a simple story over and over again.

The next four chapters form their own interconnected part of the Development Circle which we call *Shape It, Build It, Design It* and *Populate It*. These elements are explored together because they do feed off each other, but remember the creative process and development are not linear, so you can start with any of the four chapters. However, you will have to work through each of them at some point because, between them, they contain all the elements of a format. You may also need to go back to TEASER to refine your idea still further. In this *Shape It* chapter we'll look at some of the top-level decisions about your idea that help form your idea into an initial basic story shape and give you a sense of direction.

Story Shapes

Why do audiences love formats? Because, in many ways, they know what they're going to get when they watch them. And that's not a criticism. It's one of their key strengths. A really good format, like any good story, may appear simple on the screen but be warned, it is a simplicity that is hard to achieve. To just mimic that simplicity without having a great idea behind it will only give you a formula, and you don't want a formula or to be a copy. You want to create something fresh and

DOI: 10.4324/9781003050650-4

new and distinctive. We discussed what a format is in Chapter 1, but it is worth looking at it again here, especially as we have spent Chapters 2 and 3 considering creativity and ideas.

You might have already noticed how many of the formats we mention in this book have been running for a very long time. Ana de Moraes, creator of *First Dates* (Twenty Twenty/Warner Bros. Television Productions UK, 2013–present) asks her team:

> Can you imagine this running for ten years because that's what a successful format will do. Can you imagine watching this every week, bingeing on it again and again and again and still doing it in five years' time… So, a really successful format – it's something that you just want more of… that's the magic of a format – that you can repeat it forever.

We said earlier that one of the paradoxes that formats pull off is that it is the same, but different. It is endlessly repeatable, but never quite the same, and it never becomes a formula because although some of the moments are the same every week, the reactions are always different so there is still space for surprise. It is predictable in terms of knowing where you're going but not in how you'll get there.

You might be thinking but surely this is the heart of *all* storytelling, and you are not wrong. It has often been said there are only so many stories in the world and that they share the same shapes. In 1928 Vladimir Propp (1895–1970), a Russian academic, published his influential book *The Morphology of Folktales* where he brushed aside attempts to classify folktales based on themes or motifs, and explored the structure of their narratives instead. 'This explains', he said, 'the two-fold quality of a tale: its amazing multiformity, picturesqueness, and colour, and on the other hand, its no less striking uniformity, its repetition' (Propp, 1979, p. 21). The key for Propp, anyway, was in understanding that the characters were really "narrative functions". He might very well have been talking about formats!

Then in 1949 Joseph Campbell (1904–1987), building on some of Jung's insights about the power of archetypes, asked the question 'Why is mythology everywhere the same, beneath its varieties of costume?' (Campbell, 1993, p. 4) and in answer developed the concept of the Hero's Journey as an underlying pattern in mythology. In 1966 French academic Roland Barthes (1915–1980) began looking for a way to analyse narrative, 'seeking to extract from the apparent anarchy of messages, a classifying principle and a central vantage point' (Barthes, 1975, p. 238). He began from the observation that narrative was clearly not a "random assemblage of events" and thus must 'share with other narratives a common structure, open to analysis, however delicate it is to formulate' (Barthes, 1975, p. 238).

In fact, Barthes was part of the larger academic project of Structuralism which, building on the linguistics insights of Ferdinand di Saussure (1897–1913), went looking for underlying structures common to all in all sorts of disciplines and areas of culture. Many of their insights were subsequently complicated in the second half of the 20th century as post-modern perspectives on how meaning is constructed were developed. However, it is no coincidence that we draw on the Structuralist approach to narratives here because in so many ways their approach *did* reveal the simple underlying narrative structures of folk and fairy tale, and these are the same kind of straight-forward structures that appear in contemporary formats.

However, whilst Barthes and the others identified that many stories shared a relatively small number of potential "bone structures", which science-fiction novelist Kurt Vonnegut famously turned into a kind of graph (Vonnegut, 1981, p. 285ff), this remained for a long time an academic practice of analysing stories that already existed. However, being able to analyse a story is not quite the same thing as being able to create one.

The shift towards creating a "how-to" process from some of these insights seems to have begun in the 1980s and 1990s, when Christopher Vogler (b.1949) refined Campbell's ideas into a way for film and TV writers to structure their drama scripts. His book, originally titled *The Writer's Journey: Mythic Structure for Storytellers and Screenwriters* used Jung and Campbell's insights as "design principles" for storytelling, originally encapsulated in a seven-page memo written whilst working at Disney in the 1980s (Vogler, 1998, p. 31). In a similar vein, Robert McKee (b.1941), a screenwriter himself, published his influential book *Story: Substance, Structure, Style and the Principles of Screenwriting* in 1997, based on the seminar he had begun teaching in 1983 at the University of Southern California, after a stint writing for theatre, television and film. His book begins with a number of principles, the most pertinent of which for us here is 'Story is about eternal, universal forms, not formulas' (McKee, 1997, p. 3). Whilst Christopher Booker (1937–2019) began his 2004 book *The Seven Basic Plots: Why We Tell Stories* (Booker, 2004) with a discussion about how the film *Jaws* (1977, Steven Spielberg) and the eighth-century Anglo-Saxon poem *Beowulf* were related to each other, at least from a narrative structure point of view.

All these theorists and story experts make it clear that whilst there might be a smallish number of basic narrative forms, there are an almost infinite variety of ways for them to play out. That is why we can watch the same *type* of story over and over again – we all tend to have genre preferences in our movie choices, for example. We like predictability and repetition, but we also like them delivered in a way that will surprise and excite us because as Robert McKee also said an 'audience prays for surprise, the reversal of expectation' (McKee, 1997, p. 355). And this is just as true in a format as a drama. We quite like to guess what we think will happen and then be surprised when it takes a different turn. Just often enough to keep us on our toes. Illustrating the "same but different" paradox we talked about in Chapter 1.

So, what's at the heart of that repeatability? What brings people back time and time again? And what exactly is it that is repeating? What are the story shapes that work best for formats?

There are many ways to define the stories that lie beneath formats, and we'll get into some of the details in Chapter 5, but we want to take a macro view at this stage. Shape, for us, is about the fundamental purpose of the story. What are the key components that hold it together? Nell Butler, creator of *Come Dine with Me* (ITV Studios, 2005–present) suggested that 'Humans like formatting things' and 'that sport is the original format because you take real people and you put them into a situation with a set of fixed rules and you see how they get on…' And that's what a format does too. It puts people in a situation with a set of fixed rules. It's that blend of real people with the fixed rules that make a format and delivers that "same but different" paradox every time.

Popular Format Story Shapes: The Three "Cs"

We're going to look at some of the common shapes that formats take and highlight some of the main components so you can see how they work in each area, but before we do that let's lay out what we're looking for at this stage:

- A format needs a hook – some form of insight that gets people interested in the subject area (see Chapter 3).
- They also need a driver – something that powers through to the end and demands an answer.
- There also needs to be some kind of underlying tension that keeps people interested throughout the 30, 45 or 60 minutes of the show and contributes to those elements of surprise.

To explore this further, we suggest that there are three main types of formats – Competition formats, Change formats and Choice formats. These three areas, and the further sub-types we discuss, are not intended as a hard and fast categorisation of formats through hard and fast genre rules but rather as a foundation to start from.

In Chapter 1 we discussed the problems that arise when trying to place cultural works (like TV programmes) into categories using strict genre rules because they tend towards "fuzziness" at the edges. In terms of formats, this fuzziness shows up time and again because the fundamental nature of formats is one of hybridity: real people are put into constructed situations. In academia this led to a long debate about the nature of "Reality TV" versus documentary [see e.g. Escoffery (2006), Kavka (2012) and Hill (2015)], though the constructed nature of formats is now better understood by the audience (and academics). We introduce the three "Cs" here as a way to focus development, rather than as a form of analysis, and whilst we have no doubt that you will have your own ideas about such categories, let's use them for now to find and focus the central purpose of your storytelling structure.

Competition Formats

The fundamental question in these types of show is – who will win? Their story shape is designed to answer that question. Competitions are popular because they give a show a natural inbuilt driver all the way to the end of the story.

Regardless of what else is going on across an episode or a series, the audience will always want to know who wins. Jonathan Meenagh says that popular factual entertainment shows need a "pass/fail device" in every scene that shows 'whether something has worked or not worked' but, in the case of Competition formats, this "pass/fail device" extends to the whole show, and by the end it is clear to the audience what has happened, who has won or not and how they did it.

Competition formats in the form of quizzes were some of the earliest formats, as we discussed in Chapter 1, although talent competitions were also extremely popular, linking as they did to a pre-broadcast era. As Holmes notes,

> The talent show has a complex, cross-media history, given that amateur talent competitions were part of music hall and other leisure contexts such as pubs, holiday camps, "end of pier" contests and working-class cinemas in the 1930s before the advent of broadcasting.
>
> (Holmes, 2014, p. 25)

Opportunity Knocks (1949; ABC Weekend Television/ITV, 1956–1968; Thames Television, 1968–1978; BBC, 1987–1990) is often seen as one of the most interesting, with a long and complex life, beginning on BBC radio in 1949, switching between the BBC and commercial broadcasters along the way, but there were plenty of others alongside it, on radio in the 1930s and later on television, such as *New Faces* (ATV/Central/ITV Studios) which ran in several iterations between 1973 and 1988. In more recent times, Competition formats have been extended to all sorts of areas of skill, fortitude and challenge, from the physical endurance of *SAS: Who Dares Wins* (Minnow Films, 2015–present) to the crafters tasked with creating miniature masterpieces in *The Great Big Tiny Design Challenge* (Yeti Films, 2022).

In fact, we break down Competition formats into six sub-categories: Survive Something; Make Something; Perform Something; Enclosed World; Other People's Lives and Quizzes, which you can explore in more detail in Table 4.1. We suggest six here, but, of course, you may be able to think of other ways of categorising them. What we have done is to highlight the hook, and the driver as well as the underlying tension in each one. Each programme within a sub-category is very different from each other in terms of how the competition might play out but there are some common aspects to look out for.

Competition formats can go on for many series because there is always a new cast of characters with every series, and every Competition format has a range of challenges within it and ends with a winner. The story can unfold on an episode-by-episode basis or can also sit across a series. Many shows combine both aspects – they have a winner or loser each week and then an overall winner at the end of the series.

Table 4.1 sets out our interpretation of the key components of some popular shows in the competition category. We expect that you will have your own ideas about ones we have missed!

Table 4.1 Common Competition Format Shapes

Common Competition Shapes	Description	For Example	Hook	Driver	Underlying Tension
Survive Something	Participants face a major challenge, one that will push them to their *physical* limits (though often emotional limits too).	*Naked and Afraid* (Renegade 83, 2013–present) *The Jump* (Two four/Motion Content Group, 2014–2017) *The Island with Bear Grylls* (Shine TV/Banijay, 2014–present) *SAS: Who Dares Wins* (Minnow Films, 2015–present).	How can we show how difficult it is to survive in…?	Who is still standing at the end?	Can participants push past fears/do they have the strength, ability, belief and sometimes skill?
Make Something	Contestants will already have a skill, though usually at an amateur level, and compete to see who is best, according to the rules of the show and the judges. There may be a range of experience on offer, but everyone has an element of skill. The focus is on the craft itself as well as the participants. Many of these lead to celebrity or professionals or junior versions such as *Celebrity Masterchef* (Banijay, 2006–present) or *Junior Bake Off* (Love Productions, 2011–present).	*The Great British Bake Off* (Love Productions, 2010–present) *Portrait/Landscape Artist of the Year* (Storyvault Films, 2013–present) *The Great Pottery Throw Down* (Love Productions, 2015–present) *Glow Up: Britain's Next Make-Up Star* (Wall to Wall Media, 2019–present) *Interior Design Masters* (DSP/Banijay, 2019–present) *The Great Big Tiny Design Challenge* (Yeti Films, 2022).	How can we show who is the best in a popular skill?	Who will win each round, who will go home each week and who will win overall?	Competing in various tasks that challenge or show off their skills.

Shape It   47

Perform Something	The main focus is a build up to a live performance in front of a live audience, either in the studio or to an audience at home or both, and that pressure is one of the main tests for the contestants.	*The X Factor* (Syco Entertainment/Fremantle, 2004–2018, UK version) *Strictly Come Dancing* (BBC Studios, 2004–present) *Dancing on Ice* (ITV Productions, 2006–present) *The Voice* (Talpa/Lifted Entertainment, 2012–present, UK version) *The Masked Singer* (Bandicoot, 2020–present).	How can we show others doing and being the extraordinary?	The challenge of live performances and also, who will win.	Building up to the live performance, satisfying the audience and being judged.
Enclosed World	Everyone is in a specifically designed world for a relatively long period of time. Content involves interaction within the group as well as additional challenges put in by the production team throughout the time period.	*Big Brother* (Endemol Shine Group, 2000–2018) *I'm a Celebrity: Get Me out of Here* (ITV Studios, 2002–present) *Coach Trip*, (12 Yard, 2005–present) *Love Island* (ITV Studios/Lifted Entertainment, 2015–present)	How can we show how difficult it is in a limited constructed world…?	Who will stay and who will win?	How they interact and deal with extra challenges and each other?
Other People's Lives	These often tend to be stripped across a week and are a group of people who judge each other on the same subject. It may be to do with a business or with a hobby they all share.	*Four in a Bed* (Studio Lambert, 2010–present) *Come Dine with Me* (ITV Studios, 2005–present) *Take a Hike* (Cardiff Productions, 2021–present)	How can we judge ourselves in relation to other's lives?	Who wins on points or other criteria?	Snooping about, judging each other, what is being used to judge each other.
Quizzes	Quizzes and game shows. In this book we don't focus very heavily on quizzes and game shows, but it would be odd not to mention them in a section about competitions, if only because they show how competitions work so brilliantly. They are, after all, the original formats.	*Mastermind* (BBC Studios/Hat Trick Productions, 1972–present) *University Challenge* (Granada/Lifted Entertainment, 1962–present) *Pointless* (Remarkable Television, 2009–present) *Ninja Warrior UK* (Potato, 2015–present).	How can we have fun testing ourselves against others?	Who will win the prizes?	Do I have the answers, can I beat the clock, can I beat the other team, am I good enough?

However, we should inject a note of caution here. Just identifying that your idea is about someone winning something does not mean you've come up with a successful Competition format. All you have is an overall shape. It's the heart at the core of the idea, the mix of characters and the story world that makes each Competition format distinctive and it is a good hook or insight that will make it really stand out, and *because* they are such a popular form, the pressure to find one that is fresh and will succeed is intense!

Change Formats

The second major shape is that of the Change format where we see someone or something undergoing a change or makeover. Change shows are fundamentally about some kind of transformation (big or small), and we must *see* that transformation play out on the screen. The predictable bit is that we know there will be a change, but the surprise is how it develops across the show.

Of course, change is fundamental to any story, but it is particularly foregrounded in shows that have traditionally been called makeover shows. These often follow a rags-to-riches type of story (think of traditional stories like Cinderella or Pygmalion) and the audience is primarily watching to see that big reveal or change moment. The heart of this shape of format is that something major will be changed for the participants, and they can be further sub-divided in terms of the person or thing that is transformed. We identify four: Property, Person, Business and Objects.

Some of the earliest Change formats had property at their core. For example, *Ground Force* (Endemol, 1997–2005) and *Changing Rooms* (Endemol Shine UK, 1996–2004) which ran for 17 series and was then rebooted in 2021 for Channel 4. Another show that focussed on putting right things that had gone wrong was *DIY SOS* (BBC Studios 1999–2010 when it was rebooted as *DIY SOS: The Big Build*), followed by *How Clean Is Your House* (Talkback Productions, 2003–2009). However, more recently, property makeovers have shifted in another direction, this time towards making the most of what is already there, such as decluttering *Tidying Up with Marie Kondo* (The Jackal Group, 2019), lifestyles *The Minimalists: Less Is Now* (Booklight Productions, 2021) or renovations *The Restoration Man* (Tiger Aspect, 2010–present).

Another durable strand of the Change format has been the makeover show, focussing on how people look or dress, with shows such as *What Not to Wear* (BBC, 2001–2007) and *10 Years Younger* (Maverick Television, 2004–present), but there was a subsequent move towards fitness and health more generally such as *You Are What You Eat* (Celador, 2004–2006) which was rebooted by Channel 5 in 2022. In 2004 *Supernanny* (Ricochet South, 2004–2008) came along to ostensibly "makeover" children, though of course it was really the parents who needed Jo Frost's help. The show continued for seven seasons in its US version till 2011, and then for a further eighth season in 2020.

As Table 4.2 makes clear, there are also Change formats related to businesses, where a business in trouble is thrown a lifeline, often by named professional talent, such as *Ramsay's Kitchen Nightmares* (Granada/Optomen, 2004–2014) or *Mary Queen of Shops* (Optomen, 2007–2009).

Then there are Change formats focussing on the careful repair of disused and damaged items. *The Repair Shop* (Richochet, 2017–present) is a cosy programme where precious family heirlooms are carefully restored. It has itself transformed from a 30-minute daytime show on BBC2 to a 60-minute primetime slot on BBC1, and regularly features in the top 20 ratings for the week. Online there are a significant number of YouTube channels, for example, devoted to restoration videos of various kinds, some with several million subscribers. For example, *Baumgartner Restoration* (www.youtube.com/c/BaumgartnerRestoration, 2016–present), based on the work carried out in a painting restoration studio in Chicago, which has over one and a half million subscribers, and *My Mechanic* (www.youtube.com/c/mymechanics/, 2018–present) based in Switzerland, alternates restorations with builds, and has over three million subscribers.

As we can see, Change formats have evolved over the years, perhaps responding more directly to generational shifts and lifestyle changes and trends than the Competition formats for instance.

Table 4.2 sets out the four common Change format shapes.

Choice Formats

The final story shape that formats tend to fall into involves individuals or groups making a decision of some kind, sometimes several times in the same show. The fundamental focus of the show is the choice and decision (and not the resulting transformation), and sometimes that choice, and explanation for the choice, happens over and over again in the same episode. We identify four particularly popular sub-types as Isn't it Romantic, covering the ever popular dating shows from *Blind Date* (LWT, 1985–2003) to *Naked Attraction* (Studio Lambert, 2016–present); Bag a Bargain, exploring buying and selling formats such as *Four Rooms* (Talkback Thames/Boundless, 2012–2019) and *Flog It* (BBC Studios, 2002–present); All on the House covering shows such as *Location, Location, Location* (IWC Media, 2000–present); and finally Doing Business where the focus is not on a business turning a corner with the right advice (which would, of course, be a Change format) but instead focusses on the search for investment.

Choice formats usually involve areas that we can all relate to – romance, business, selling things – areas that don't need a lot of setup because we recognise what lies at the core of them in our everyday lives. Not everyone has a tattoo, but everyone has done something they regret. Not everyone has a business to invest in, but everyone has had to persuade someone to spend money on something – even if it is just agreeing on what takeaway to buy whilst watching TV. So, these often need less setup because the premise becomes familiar very quickly – but, because of this, the premise needs to be something easily understood.

Table 4.3 sets out four sub-types of Choice formats.

We have no doubt that you will be looking at some of our examples and thinking "ah, yes but…" and coming up with shows that might fit into more than

50 Shape It

Table 4.2 Common Change Format Shapes

Common Change Format Shapes	Description	For Example	Hook	Driver	Underlying Tension
Property	Although there are people involved, the change is focussed on a property or physical space. The participants themselves may not see all the change happening before the final reveal or they may be doing the work themselves.	*Changing Rooms* (Endemol Shine UK, 1996–2004, 2021) *How Clean Is Your House* (Talkback Productions, 2003–2009) *The Restoration Man* (Tiger Aspect, 2010–present) *The Minimalists: Less Is Now* (Booklight Productions, 2021) *Sort Your Life Out with Stacey Solomon* (Optomen Productions, 2021–present) *Extraordinary Extensions* (Avalon, 2021–present)	How can we show a transformed space for a better life?	What will be changed?	Will the participants compromise?
Person	These shows look at aspects of individuals or families ready to make a change. Sometimes it is straightforward in terms of appearance, sometimes a little more challenging in terms of behaviour and habits, but either way the audience must still be able to see the transformation.	*What Not to Wear* (BBC, 2001–2007) *10 Years Younger* (Maverick Television, 2004–present). *Snog Marry Avoid* (Remarkable Television, 2008–2013) *Tattoo Fixers* (Studio Lambert, 2015–2019) *This Time Next Year* (ITV Studios, 2016–2019) *Queer Eye* (Scout Productions, 2018–present)	How can we show a personal transformation happening?	How will they change?	How far will participants go? How they react to the changes suggested?

Business	A failing business is given a shot in the arm, usually by a professional talent.	*Ramsay's Kitchen Nightmares* (Granada/Optomen, 2004–2014) *Mary Queen of Shops* (Optomen, 2007–2009) *Mary Portas Secret Shopper* (Optomen, 2011–2016)	How can we show the path to business success?	Will the business be saved?	Will the participants take the advice?
Object	An object, sometimes valuable, is given a new lease of life through careful restoration.	*The Repair Shop* (Richochet, 2017–present) *My Mechanics*, Youtube, 2018–present) *Baumgartner Restoration*, (Youtube, 2016–present) *re.anything* (TikTok) *Saved and Remade* (Red Sky Productions Ltd, 2021–present)	How can we make it as good as new?	Will the process work?	Can it be fixed or made useful again? What are the stages that the item has to go through?

52 Shape It

Table 4.3 Common Choice Format Shapes

Common Choice Format Shapes	Description	For Example	Hook	Driver	Underlying Tension
Isn't It Romantic?	These programmes are often based around dating rules or various rituals around romance that are well recognised – a dinner or a dance or leading up to something like a wedding.	*Blind Date* (LWT, 1985–2003) *First Dates* (Twenty Twenty/Warner Bros. Television Productions UK, 2013–present) *Naked Attraction* (Studio Lambert, 2016–present) *Take Me Out*, (Thames, 2010–2019) *Say Yes to the Dress* (Half Yard Productions, 2016–2017) *Married at First Sight* (CPL Productions, 2015–present)	How can we make the right choice or find "the one"? How can we find love?	Will they choose the right person?	How to choose who to date?
Bag a Bargain	Everyone loves a bargain. This story shape is either about finding bargains or not getting cheated. They are often daytime formats.	*Antiques Roadshow* (BBC Studios, 1979–present) *Cash in the Attic* (Leopard Films, 2002–2012) *Flog It* (BBC Studios, 2002–present) *Four Rooms* (Talkback Thames/Boundless, 2012–2019)	How can we bag a bargain?	Will it be worth more than they paid for it? Is it really a bargain?	Finding value and worth, the bargain, the purchase.
All on the House	There is no doubt that formats reflect a nation's obsession. The shows here are focussed on the choice of to buy or not to buy, or whether to buy at all.	*Location, Location, Location* (IWC Media, 2000–present) *A Place in the Sun* (Freeform Productions, 2000–present). *Escape to the Country* (Naked, 2002–present) *Wanted Down Under* (BBC, 2007–present) *Tiny House Nation* (Loud TV, 2014–2019)	How can we choose another, better place to live?	Did they buy it, which one did they buy?	Will they compromise, and what information helps them make a decision?

Doing Business	These shows usually feature participants seeking investment or help for a business. The focus is on an investor choosing whether to make an offer or the owner choosing to accept.	*Dragon's Den* (BBC Studios, 2005–present) *Undercover Boss* (Studio Lambert, 2009–2014, but remains in production around the world.) *The Profit* (CNBC, 2013–2021)	Can we show how to persuade someone to hand over cash or help with your business?	Will they be persuasive enough, is it good enough for investment? Will they take the offer?	Needing help to start or improve the business and take it to the next level but there may be compromise involved.

one category and so on, but remember these categories are not intended to be applied as strict rules, but rather as potential story shapes for your own idea. So, if you are asking questions about how they work and what is at stake, then you are already starting to think in the right way.

And Then There Was One…

There is always at least one idea that doesn't quite fit into any category. We said in Chapter 3 that the television industry tends towards incremental innovation, except when it doesn't! There is always room for something new, for the next big thing, something no one expected.

Gogglebox (Studio Lambert, 2013–present) defies description in the context of the above. It features different groups of people watching television from the comfort of their own homes. There's nothing at stake for them (except possible fallout from a badly worded reaction but that comes after the event, not during the show); they never interact with each other; they don't react to anything in the outside world only to what's happening on the screen in front of them. It certainly feels more like something you'd see on social media or on a streaming platform, but it is a television review show and there is no doubt that it works. In the words of Stephen Lambert: 'it's a show about a collection of characters you get to know and sort of love, and it's cut for their emotional engagement with what they're watching, whether it's a comedic reaction or a dramatic reaction'.

This is to remind you that although these story shapes are helpful when it comes to starting to structure an idea, there is always room for something else. But don't disregard them either. The majority of shows still fit into those categories.

So far, we have sketched out some of the most successful story shapes for formats, and perhaps one of them has already jumped out at you, but maybe you're still not sure which shape fits your idea best. This exercise is going to offer you some ways to help clarify that decision.

Exercise: Start at the End

The clearest way to work out which shape will work is to think about your ending. Where and how does your story end? If there is a winner, then it's a Competition format. If it is about seeing something or someone changed at the end, then it fits into the Change formats. If there are multiple answers throughout – the Dragons bid, or they don't – then it is a choice show.

You might be hesitating because people will often change whilst going through a competition, and often that change is what keeps people watching. It is certainly important, but in terms of structure and story shape, if you are whittling down the numbers until there is only one winner at the end, it is a Competition format. Change and Choice often overlap too. A toy is certainly changed once it is repaired. An antique that was worthless is changed if valued differently. Someone's life is changed if they're given money to grow their business.

A body is changed when a tattoo is removed. However, what makes it a choice show is that the focus is on the moment of decision and not on the big reveal or transformation.

Each of the three major forms outlined above is driven by its own very simple question.

- Competition – who will win?
- Change – how will this [person, property, business, object] be changed?
- Choice – what will the decision be?

Take your concept from Chapter 3, or perhaps your hook from the TEASER Grid, and try putting it into *each* of these categories or sub-categories. What would it look like if it had a live element or drove to a big performance? How would it look in an Enclosed World? How could you show a transformation? At this point you still want to stay flexible, stay curious and keep exploring. How does your idea change in different categories? What options does it open up or close down? And don't ignore those negative reactions. It's worth just as much to think "oh no, definitely not that" as it is to know what you *do* want.

This decision about the shape drives your story. Once you put your subject and the key driver together you have created what Gerard Costello terms a "pact with the viewer" – a pact that you have made

> at the beginning of the programme and you must deliver on by the end. If you don't then your format has failed. And then it has to be able to deliver this regularly, episode in, episode out, series in, series out.

Having thought about the type of story that might suit your idea, and what pact you want to make with your audience, we now move on to some of the other major considerations for shaping a format at the start of the process.

Building the Contours

The format is beginning to take shape, but there are few more top-level decisions you can make at this stage that help to shape the direction of travel for your idea – the setting, agency and story arcs.

Whenever you construct a story, your audience enters it for the duration of that story. This is particularly obvious in drama, where you might think of the world of *Game of Thrones* (HBO, 2011–2019), or the planets of the *Star Wars* franchise (Lucasfilm Ltd). For these fantasy and science-fiction dramas, the audience obviously enter another world, one based on a fantasy history, or one based on imaginary planets possibly in the future, but it is equally true of any story. The audience is always invited into a world where there are set rules and where the participants in the show abide by those rules, whether it is that "dragons exist", "faster than light travel is possible" or "you must bake a cake". Formats, too, must set up their own "story world".

We will discuss the design elements of building that story world in Chapter 6, but for now there is still a decision to be made about "where". It might seem like there could be an infinite number of answers but can in fact be summed up as a choice of three: the Ordinary World, a Studio World and an Enclosed World.

Some shows are set in the familiar ordinary world, on location, in real life. Much of the visual appeal of *Race Across the World* and *Take a Hike* comes from the audience travelling along with the contestants. Others do take place in the "real world" but it is really only a version of that real world. Remember that formats are a form of "constructed reality" rather than pure documentary, so bear in mind once again that "real but not real" paradox from Chapter 1.

First Dates takes us to a lovely (and real) restaurant where love might be on the menu, but with helpful, interested waiting staff ready with an encouraging word. *The Repair Shop* is full of highly skilled workers who can fix any of your cherished items – but what are the chances in the real world that they are all in the same place at the same time? *Come Dine with Me* is set in other people's houses but not many people normally go to five dinner parties a week – at least, we don't! As Richard McKerrow explained,

> you take things that are already happening, and you blow them up. Television offers you this opportunity… to blow it up into something bigger and magical… in a way, it's like being a novelist… *Bake Off* is a magical realism form. But the really difficult thing… it's all about keeping it real.

So even formats set in the "real world" still offer a kind of heightened reality version of the everyday. They are not, as we keep saying, documentary.

A Studio World offers much greater control as the production usually build what it needs in the form of a set. *Masterchef* primarily takes place in a studio set, with no audience. *Strictly Come Dancing* is filmed at Elstree Studios, with an invited audience, except when it goes on location to the Blackpool Tower Ballroom. *Ninja Warrior UK* (Potato, 2015–present) is filmed on a specially made studio in Manchester Central Convention Complex. Gameshows and some dating shows too, such as *Naked Attraction*, take place in a studio setting.

Sometimes the ordinary worlds and the studio worlds can exist in a hybrid form. For example, *The Great British Bake Off* and *Strictly Come Dancing* allow the normal world to appear through phone calls or visits to studio in order to provide support, whilst others use the ordinary world as an additional challenge – as in *Hunted* where one of the rules is that they have to make contact with their family or use the cash machine. They have to stay hidden in the real world rather than escape into another one. In transformation or makeover shows such as *Queer Eye* we need to see their current world so we can understand and appreciate the change that the change makers help bring into being. (*Queer Eye* was originally a Bravo Original Production/Scout Productions show called *Queer Eye for the Straight Guy*, running from 2003 to 2007 before being rebooted for Netflix in 2018.)

In some formats the ordinary world doesn't get a look in as we dive straight down the rabbit hole, straight into the extraordinary. In the Enclosed World shows the participants are cut off completely from the outside world and kept in a bubble for the duration, as there is a risk that bursting that bubble may burst the whole concept of the world and therefore the programme. We don't always see the participants at home beforehand or find out much about their lives outside the world they're entering. It's like a time outside of time, it exists within its own constraints. You might think something like *SAS: Who Dares Wins* is an Ordinary World type of show since it is filmed on location, but it is really an Enclosed World every bit as much as *Big Brother*, as the recruits are totally immersed in the military environment for the duration of their time on the show.

Exercise: Where in the World?

What kind of world does your story take place in? Or if that is too big a question for the moment, turn it around and ask which world do you think your idea might fit into?

- The Ordinary World or even the Real World – but bear in mind it is still a version of that with constraints and rules such as an enhanced time frame or with experts coming to help out in a way that they wouldn't in normal life. If only we could all have two experienced property experts finding our homes for us whenever we needed them, or five experts overhauling our life.
- A Studio World – a specially constructed set. The action might break out of it from time to time. *The Voice* (Talpa/Lifted Entertainment, 2012–present, UK version) has rehearsal rooms, for example, and *Strictly Come Dancing* may visit other places to inspire the celebrities, but it's all leading back to that studio.
- An Enclosed World – where everything takes place in that world.

You might feel that one of these is a more natural fit but stay flexible and work it through. What happens to your idea if you put it into another type of world? Try them all on for size.

But You Do Make the Rules

We reminded you above that formats are "constructed reality" that demonstrate the "real but not real" paradox, but the story world isn't created just by the setting alone. It is also constructed by the rules you create to frame it and create the action. Remember that formats are designed to reliably, simply and repeatedly generate stories. As Richard McKerrow put it, 'You set up a frame and what I call a world and there are rules within that world', and all stories benefit from having some boundaries. That's what formats specialise in – creating the boundaries or rules. It may look as though there are no rules but there are always rules. It's just that they are on a spectrum from the more obvious in the case of competitions, to the less obvious, in the case of Change formats.

For example, in *Hunted* Jonathan Meenagh noted they were aware of one big problem: 'we called it the Barry scenario – what would you do if [the contestant] went to Barry's flat in Wales in the hills somewhere and… lived in the attic for four weeks'. That may be the best way to go on the run in reality, but it would make for a very dull TV show. So, as Meenagh went on to explain,

> that's one of the rules of the show, you can only stay somewhere for a certain amount of time. You have to take money out of the bank every forty-eight hours and using *this* card… so that you're leaving a trace.

He calls them an "array of trigger points" – moments which alert the authorities who are in pursuit of them and set off a "cat and mouse" chase. This is one of the major ways that formats differ from documentaries. You set the rules in place.

Nell Butler suggests a useful way to think about this aspect of format development. She said,

> it is useful to work out whether you're trying to make a really tight format or a loose format. Once you've got that in your head then you have a better sense of what your options are, … what you want to control and what you want to just surprise you.

So, you might be thinking about a heavily formatted show where it is really clear what the rules are, and both the participants and the audience can see those rules. An example of this is the technical challenge in *The Great British Bake Off* where we know that the contestants have been given a set task and an allotted amount of time to complete it, though the participants do then have freedom to react to the constraints. Or you can put only few rules in place and then leave room for what happens next. For example, the producers of *First Dates* choose their participants, introduce two people to each other, arrange for them to have a meal together, then film the resulting interactions. They don't tell them what to talk about whereas in *Eating with my Ex* (Fremantle Media, 2017–present), the questions are prompted by messages delivered with their plates.

Most shows do a mix of both, but it is worth considering the relative balance. Do you leave space for more reaction or tightly control what happens next, because what you don't want is for things to be so constructed that there is no room for natural reaction. That can sometimes happen because you want to be sure that there are enough things happening to make sure you can fill the time, but as Caroline Roseman said,

> When we first pitched *Ex On The Beach*, it had a lot more format beats. MTV believed that the core premise and hook of the show was so strong that it didn't have to be so constructed. I was quite married to those format beats at

the time, so it was tough to let some of them go – but they were absolutely right. When a show has a strong enough topline and great casting, then the stories will carry the show. Story is king. Especially within the reality genre.

Exercise: Who's in Control?

In quite general terms, consider the number of rules, format points, tasks, interviews or whatever you think you need to get to your endpoint. We do come back to these in more detail in Chapter 5, so keep it quite general for now. The more points you have, the tighter the format will be.

Now consider how much agency will you allow your participants? How important is the reaction of your participants? The more space for reaction, the looser the format will be. This is something we will come back to in more detail in Chapter 7.

Taking both of these perspectives into account, along with the proposed length of an episode, roughly where would you place your idea on a spectrum of tight/highly formatted to loose/lightly formatted?

Story Dispensing

The final top-level decision to think about at this stage is whether you are going to be building a story across multiple episodes, or is each story complete in one episode. An "arc" in general terms forms part of a curving trajectory, like an arrow or a javelin shot through the air, and when it is used in terms of story, it is used to denote that same sense of movement. As one writer puts it, 'A true narrative arc sweeps forward across time, pushing ahead with constant motion. It looks like a wave about to break, a pregnant package of stored energy' (Hart, 2011, pp. 25–26). So, a narrative arc implies story-in-movement, and relates to how much information (story) there is to tell, and how it is dispensed across time. It is interesting that in Propp's analysis of the simple folktale, one of his key observations was that the elements of the story could only be used in the same order: the story could only be constructed by moving forwards.

Whilst we will be talking more about the building blocks of "story" in Chapter 5, at this stage of top-level decisions there is still an important choice to be made. Will your show tell its story across one episode – that is, as a closed story arc in discrete episodes – or will the story be told across multiple episodes in a series arc? How will your story be dispensed across time?

Competition formats on the whole lend themselves well to a series arc, but quiz shows and gameshows more often start and end in the same episode. Streaming services have led a push for more series arcs, because they want to keep audiences binge watching. As Caroline Roseman explained,

> streamer development is quite different from network show development in that they want their shows, especially in dating reality… to almost feel like

a ten-hour movie rather than ten standalone episodes. ... they want people to binge watch these shows and so they don't like any episode to feel like it has a beginning and an end.

An SVOD might even choose to end an episode mid-scene to keep people watching.

Some formats are structured a little like chapters in the overall series. For example, *Come Dine with Me* or *Take a Hike* are often stripped across a week (meaning it is on every day), where you are with the same group of people for four or five episodes, and then follow a different group of people the following week. Other shows are complete stories in a single episode and for this type of show, continuity across the series is provided more by the setup and the judges, presenters or experts. Change formats often fall into this category as we watch one person, or one business, undergo a transformation in one episode. In some shows, episodes can be sub-divided even further into mini-story arcs, such as *The Repair Shop*, where the audience will follow the restoration of three or four objects interwoven across the hour, or in a Choice format like *Dragon's Den* (BBC Studios, 2005–present) the investors will hear sometimes five or six pitches in a single episode in a linear way.

Exercise: What Is the Trajectory?

Consider whether your idea can sustain interest and excitement over multiple episodes, or whether it will be punchier in smaller doses? How will you keep interest and excitement on the way to answering your fundamental question who will win, who will be transformed, who will make a decision?

Does your idea suit a closed episode, a series arc or mini arcs? As before, try them all for size. Really take the time to work it through and think about what you would need to do to make it work in a single episode or across a series.

Back Round Again

Before we dive into Chapter 5 and start to build the details of the story, it is worth reflecting back to the insights from Chapter 3 and once again considering what your story is really about. You've been thinking your way through a lot of issues since we last considered your hook. Maybe your idea is about winning a skills test, but is it really about confidence? Or nostalgia? Or bravery? Because, if you can identify something bigger about your story that will help with all the other aspects still to come, such as why it might appeal to people to take part in it, and does it help you decide where to set it, or how to end it? "Are you looking for love?" is the question Ana de Moraes asked prospective participants for *First Dates*. Jonathan Mcenagh asks 'What am I going to understand more about myself when I watch that… It's not just a series of events … what's driving it and what's the human question at the base'. It's got to be *about* something.

Exercise: Yes, but What Is It *Really* About?

If stories are about exploring the world around us, then what is your idea exploring? You might want to go back to your original insight and the TEASER Grid.

Note down some of the things you think your idea is really about. Then look back at everything you have decided so far and write out your big-ticket decisions in one line.

This is a [x] format, set in a [x] world, told across [x] episodes and is really about [x].

To get started you could practice with some shows you know. For example:

Interior Design Masters (DSP/Banijay, 2019–present) is a "make something" Competition format, set in the real world (mostly), told across eight episodes and is really about taste.

Wheeler Dealers (Betty/All3Media, 2003–present) is an Object Change format, set in the real world, told across one episode and is really about love of classic cars.

Escape to the Country (Naked, 2002–present) is a Choice format, set in the real world, told across one episode and is really about the path not taken.

In this chapter we moved round the Development Circle with some big decisions about the fundamental story shape of your idea. Formats are great stories and like all stories they are driven by three key elements: the hook we use to appeal to audiences to watch; the key driver which is the single question which the audience want to be answered by the end of the episode or series; and the underlying tension, a series of twists and turns, that will keep audiences engaged throughout.

Whilst there isn't widespread industry agreement on a definitive list of format types, we have chosen three fundamental shapes to focus on: Competition, Change and Choice. Competition is about survival in a real or enclosed world, being the best at making, performing or even in how you live your life. Change is about how to improve life, either through our own skills or the use of others' skills, improving personally, property or a community, business or even an object. Choice involves the life choices we all make and whether we win or lose based on our decisions; whether this is in love, big or small purchases, or what we invest in life.

Then we considered three additional big-ticket items concerning where the action might take place; how tight or loose your "rules" might be; and finally, how your story might be doled out across one episode or many, before circling back around the question of deeper themes that might attract your audience.

You can see how far you have come already from those first half-formed thoughts in Chapter 2. But keep going – in Chapter 5 you'll find out how to build in even more detail to keep your story moving forward.

References

Barthes, R., 1975, An Introduction to the Structural Analysis of Narrative, *New Literary History*, 6(2), pp. 237–272.

Booker, C., 2004, *Seven Basic Plots: Why We Tell Stories*, London, Continuum.
Campbell, J. 1993, *Hero with a Thousand Faces*. London, Fontana Press.
Escoffery, D., 2006, *How Real Is Reality TV?: Essays on Representation and Truth*, McFarland & Co, North Carlina, Jefferson.
Hart, J., 2011, *Storycraft: The Complete Guide to Writing Narrative Nonfiction*, Chicago, University of Chicago Press.
Hill, A., 2015, *Reality TV*, Abingdon, Routledge.
Holmes, S., 2014, 'You Don't Need Influence… All You Need Is Your First Opportunity!': The Early Broadcast Talent Show and the BBC, *Critical Studies in Television*, 9(1), pp. 23–42.
Kavka, M., 2012, *Reality TV*, Edinburgh, University of Edinburgh Press.
McKee, R., 1997, *Story: Substance, Structure, Style and the Principles of Screenwriting*, New York, HarperCollins Publishers.
Propp, V., 1979, *The Morphology of the Folk Tale*, Austin, University of Texas Press.
Vogler, C., 1998, *The Writer's Journey: Mythic Structure for Writers*, San Francisco, Michael Wiese Productions.
Vonnegut, K., 1981, *Palm Sunday: An Autobiographical Collage*, New York, Dial Press.

5 Build It

Now that you have made some top-levels decisions about the overall shape of the format, we can start looking at more story detail. Every format is different – even when two formats are a competition format, take place in an enclosed world and run across a whole series, they are still very different from each other. *Love Island* (ITV Studios/Lifted Entertainment, 2015–present), for example, is different from *Ex on the Beach* (Whizz Kid Entertainment, 2014–present) and *Love in the Flesh* (Ten66 Television, 2022), even though you might agree they are all Enclosed World Competition formats on a theme of love and dating, with swimwear!

We know formats work by creating rules that reliably result in a compelling story. As Kate Phillips, BBC Controller for Entertainment, put it, 'A format is the rules and structure you put on an idea. You have an idea, and you layer it with the structures and the rules'.

In Chapter 5 we explored the fundamental shape that lies beneath many story types, but in this chapter, we are looking at how that story actually unfolds to build in tension and excitement in a way that will be unique to your idea. You might already have decided (having worked through all the options) that you want your format to be an Enclosed World Competition, so you know where you are going, but how are you going to get there? Remember that the term "arc" implies forward movement, but what are the details – the colour, the humour, the emotion, the twists and turns – that are going to get the story and the audience moving in the right direction?

This might sound as if we are talking about drama, and we are! Formats tell stories every bit as much as the latest soap opera, it's just a simplified pared-down drama, where you aren't responsible for absolutely every single reaction of your characters. Instead, as the creator of the format, it is your job to put in place the rules to structure events and keep the story moving forward and engaging. Formats are simple stories, but the heart, the humour and the entertainment come from the real people who enter your world of story rules. This is one of those key paradoxes at the heart of a format – they are "real but not real". Your story rules engineer a succession of incidents for the participants, that flow and build and emotionally engage an audience, whether it is to make them laugh or cry. Those incidents are planned at the early stages of a format to ensure they have some kind of tension, or conflict, or challenge built in and that they build up to a

DOI: 10.4324/9781003050650-5

satisfying resolution. As John Yorke, one of the UK's most well-known television story experts, observed:

> In the early years of the new millennium TV executives finally learned this brilliant lesson – that all narrative demands a brilliant arc and that television in particular lends itself exceptionally well to its shape. They realised that by following the rules of dramatic structure but applying it to real people, they could provide on a weekly basis the visceral thrill that TV drama could only deliver sporadically.
>
> (Yorke, 2014, p. 195)

The classic way to talk about story is in terms of the Act Structure, sometimes a three-act structure, or in John Yorke's case a five-act structure, but often when discussing the smaller elements of story construction, the language used can vary quite widely. We talked about the big shape of stories in Chapter 4, and in this one we talk about story in more detail using act structures, format points and format beats, and we will define what we specifically mean by these as we go. We will come to the act structure shortly, but we want to start by considering "format points" first.

Format Points

Drama writers will often talk about plot points, a term coined by Syd Field in his seminal 1979 book *Screenplay*. He uses it to mean 'an incident, or event, that "hooks" into the action' and crucially 'moves the story forward' (Field, 1982, p. 111). It may even be a turning point that shifts the direction of the story. Story generally works through a chain of cause and effect, which audiences will try to make sense of because 'A random string of events is hard to understand as a story' (Bordwell et al, 2020, p. 73). The pattern of cause and effect is what causes the audience to consider what they are seeing as a story, and to wonder what will happen next.

In a format, this chain of cause and effect works in exactly the same way. We considered these very loosely in Chapter 4, asking you whether you thought there would be a need for a lot of them, or not so many. Format points are the key rules that are going to guarantee you action and drama. They are the crucial moments repeated in every episode because ultimately they form the basis of your format. So, format points are the story rules that engineer a succession of incidents that build the action of the format.

If you stick to thinking about the action itself for now, what are the major things you expect to happen across your story? These might be things that you already visualised when you first considered the idea, the things you know need to happen, although you might not have defined exactly *how* you want them to happen yet. For example, you might want there to be a physical task or a skills test for your Make Something Competition, but you don't know what that task is yet or where it will take place, but you do know that there has to be a skills test at some point in the show. Make a note of all the things you think should be there, even if it is still just the ending. If it's a Competition Format, there has to be a winner, right? If it's a Change format, we've got to see a reveal. A Choice format means someone has made a decision. How do the format points build the action to get us there?

We are calling these format points, but Nell Butler calls them "stepping-stones" and that is a helpful image because, as she explains, in "very tight formats" they are "mapped out very tightly" and "the stepping-stones are very close to each other" whereas in a looser format they may be further apart. How many do you need? Use your driver as a guide. If you know where you need to be at the end (one winner, a completely changed person, a new skill learned, something repaired), then what are the major steps needed for that to happen? It is helpful to think about these at as early a stage as possible.

Exercise: Stepping-Stones

You might refer back to the exercises in Chapter 4. We're really starting to build up some detail now.

- What is your ending?
- How are you going to get to the ending you identified in Chapter 4? For example, do they need to complete a task, sing a song, bring in something to be fixed, be judged, answer questions?
- What are five or six of those key stepping-stones? What are the actions (causes) that will set up the results (effect) you need?
- Do they logically follow each other in a chain of cause and effect?
- How close or far apart from each other are they? How much space do you leave for reaction?
- What would make a great starting point? What is your triggering event, or inciting incident?

We now have a series of actions that might already be falling into a good structure, with a chain of cause-and-effect actions pulling the story forward, or it might still be a bit jumbled up and in danger of being a "random string of events", but consideration of act structure can help.

A Class Act

We are going to talk about act structures now, but with a word of warning. There are a lot of different ways of talking about story structure and we think it is important not to get too hung up on the fine details because everyone gives them slightly different names. The key thing is to focus on the purpose behind them: structure brings shape to your story. Structure is fundamentally about how you tell the story – so, if you think you've got a slightly chaotic collection of possible format points, actions or "causes", take them all and think, but what does the story need to keep moving forward? Where is the chain of cause and effect that is going to pull the story through?

Here's a four-point story theory:

- You need something to start your story off.
- Things have to happen – a number of major challenges or conflicts related to the goal that you will "build up to" and "come away from" in each story.
- You don't want it to be predictable, so you need surprises and/or reversals.
- You need something to show that it has come to an end and that your character has gone through something or learned something or experienced something or won something.

In fact, this really translates to probably the most famous pattern in story – the three-act structure, first set out by Classical Greek philosopher Aristotle in *Poetics* in the fourth century BCE. 'Well-constructed plots' he wrote, 'should neither begin from a random point, nor conclude at a random point, but should use the elements we have mentioned [i.e. beginning, middle, conclusion]' (Aristotle, 1987, p. 10). Notice that although Aristotle doesn't use the terms "cause and effect", he does make the same point about plots (narrative/story) not starting and ending at random.

The three-act structure formed the basis of received wisdom about how to structure drama for centuries (along with Roman poet Horace's pitch for the five-act structure in *Ars Poetica*) (Horace & Persius, 2005). William Archer, for example, noted in his 1912 book *Play-Making: A Manual of Craftsmanship* that the three-act structure was 'certainly of enormous and invaluable convenience' (Archer, 1912, p. 137), but it was almost certainly the book *Screenplay* (1979) by Hollywood writer and producer Syd Field (1935–2013) that popularised it in screenwriting circles.

The three-act structure is still the basis of much storytelling, and since one of the defining rules of a format is that it has to be simple and easy to understand, many follow the three-act structure, which breaks down as follows:

- Act 1: set up a story world, introduce the characters and set up key problems.
- Act 2: make the situation more difficult, or pass on, or develop skills to help them solve their problem.
- Act 3: resolve the situation, win or lose, show a change, make a decision.

A quiz is a great example of a three-act drama – the host introduces the world in terms of the rules of the quiz, the contestant gets introduced, questions get harder, stakes get higher as the potential of losing grows. There's usually a twist or an escalation at some point. And then they win or lose. *Who Wants to be a Millionaire* (Sony Pictures Television, 1998–present) is a great example: as the stakes continue to rise, there is quite literally more to lose with every question asked – even in quizzes where there is little, or no money involved, there is still tension around who will win.

Let's go a bit deeper into the purpose of those acts to work out what you're looking for in each act.

> Act 1 – The purpose of the first act is to introduce the characters and the story world itself. It lays the foundations of what is to follow. Perhaps rules need to be explicitly explained, the constraints made clear and the participants introduced. Then something needs to start the story off, normally in the form of a challenge. The participant says, "I need to buy a house" and an expert or team of experts arrives to help them make their choice, as in *Location, Location, Location* (IWC Media, 2000–present), for example.
>
> Act 2 – The purpose of the second act is to create complications, reactions and further challenges. We look for some payoffs from the first questions, looking for new setups that are the consequences of earlier decisions (cause and effect). The participant needs to buy a house, but it turns out they have unrealistic expectations of how much houses cost in their top choice of location. Will they accept a smaller house or be prepared to move further afield? The middle is the bit in between leaving the starting blocks and crossing the finishing line to use a sporting analogy. In this Act, what pulls the audience along and keeps them engaged? Introduce problems, complications, surprises. This is when reality comes crashing in or where many of the decisions and difficulties your character is facing become clear. Your job is to find the right ones that help highlight the story you want to tell and keep it moving.
>
> Act 3 – It is decision time! This is where the participants have to make the decision, based on all that they've gone through or where they perform. It should be the hardest task. And there should be a resolution, as Aristotle said, your story should not 'conclude at a random point'. This is where you answer the question you set up in Act 1 and tie everything up, where you deliver on the "pact" as Gerard Costello called it. The ending should close off the chain of cause and effect. And you do need a good ending, a climax – don't just fizzle away…

As you can see each act depends on the one before. Any complications, challenges or problems that emerge as the story continues should all build on what has come before rather than stand alone. It is also the case that the three-act structure can run across a segment of an individual episode, across a complete episode or even across an entire series, regardless of how many episodes there might be.

Let's look at some examples.

Dragon's Den (BBC Studios, 2005–present) – a tightly formatted show where in fact each individual pitch follows the three-act structure.

> Act 1 – introduction to the entrepreneur and their produce or business.
> Act 2 – the participants get questioned in depth about strengths and weaknesses and plans for the future.

Act 3 – based on what is found out in previous acts, the Dragons may have decided not to invest, or the entrepreneur may have several offers to consider. A decision must be made either way.

The Repair Shop (Richochet, 2017–present) – again, each item follows the three-act structure, though the story will be interwoven with the stories of several other objects across the episode.

Act 1 – introduce the owner and their item and why it matters to them, find out which expert best suits the challenge of restoring it.
Act 2 – what are the difficulties or challenges in repairing this particular item, find out more about how repair is done.
Act 3 – reuniting the owner with their item and their response.

Wheeler Dealers (Betty/All3Media, 2003–present) – here each episode follows the three-act structure.

Act 1 – meet the car seller and the car-buying expert, discover the specific car and the key challenges of restoration.
Act 2 – the mechanic works on the car and discovers more problems, some mild disagreement between the two presenters, solutions to mechanical problems are sought.
Act 3 – the renovated and transformed car is revealed, driven and then sold.

Come Dine with Me (ITV Studios, 2005–present), a relatively loosely formatted show, where the three-act structure works in each episode, but also across the week's episodes.

Act 1 – set up world and meet all the participants, discover more about the host and their house, set up the rules.
Act 2 – the meal and reactions, to the food and each other, fussy guests, problems with the cooking, questionable entertainment, people falling out.
Act 3 – the marking and judging from everyone, until, in the final episode at the end of the week, a winner is announced.

The Apprentice (Mark Burnett Productions/Talkback Productions, 2005–present), where each episode follows the three-act structure, but it also builds to the final hiring.

Act 1 – introduce the task and key characters for that week, state of relationships.
Act 2, part 1 – the task is carried out, how it affects relationships, difficulties, challenges, etc.

Act 2, part 2 – the boardroom – who won, what the result brings out about the relationships, the consequences of what happened when they carried out the task.

Act 3 – the decision about who gets fired.

Love Island (ITV Studios/Lifted Entertainment, 2015–present), which follows the three-act structure through the whole series.

Act 1 – introductions, initial relationships, meeting the contestants, getting an idea of who they are, initial pairings, idea of where problems might arise.

Act 2 – reactions as people swap partners or find out more about each other or new people are introduced into the island. People get voted off by various means disrupting some relationships and starting others.

Act 3 – numbers reduce, tension, emotional investment as audience have got to know the people more and people until there is only one couple left.

These are summarised overviews – obviously within each episode and series there is a lot going on, but the basic principles of each act hold true. The important thing to keep in mind that anything that is set up has to get a payoff. If you set up a cause, there must be an effect or consequence. This creates the chain that pulls the narrative forward. That central driver that we explored in Chapter 4 needs a resolution, from who will win, who will they get the money, to will they get another date, or find love, or have a successful wedding?

Exercise: Act Up

Go back to the list of stepping-stones that you created in the previous exercise and start considering where they might fit into an act structure.

Act 1 – What needs set up? What is the driving question? Where are we headed?

Act 2 – How can you complicate, make more difficult, up the stakes?

Act 3 – What is resolved, plus, if you're building across a series, what is set up for the next episode? How is the chain of cause and effect brought to a close?

You should keep adding detail to these three acts throughout the rest of the book, as you layer in casting decisions and elements of design.

Keep the Beat

We now come to the smallest element of the story structure, the "format beat". One of the key things when looking at developing a format is to see if the central in-built conflict is enough to sustain "the same but different paradox" across a number of series. A lot of this comes from the underlying tension that you identified in the Chapter 4 or in the insight from TEASER. The tension has to be significant and important enough to keep audiences hooked. For example, in a Choice format property show like *Location, Location, Location* or *A Place in the Sun* (Freeform Productions, 2000–present) it is exactly the same tension every time – will the participants find a property they like, and will they decide to buy it? This is something an audience happily watches over and over again because the participants and the houses are different every time.

In all these cases, a "simple" tension is repeated, but it is how the participants act and react that makes the difference. Robert McKee describes a "story beat" as the smallest element of structure, but a beat, he says, 'is an exchange of behaviour in action/reaction. Beat by Beat these changing behaviours shape the turning of a scene' (McKee, 1997, p. 37). We have emphasised the idea of "cause and effect" as a way of driving a story forward, but McKee argues that reaction is just as, if not more, important because that is how the next action is set up. We discover a lot about someone by their reactions to a situation or challenge. Some people get frustrated if they don't do as well as they wanted or if they are paired with someone they don't like; other people can use that frustration as a spur to action or are more relaxed about it. So, the actions and reactions of your participants, judges, presenters or experts, are not something peripheral to the story. Along with the actions you set up in the format points, these format beats are also a vital part of how the story moves forward.

In a format you need to provide enough format points to make the story happen, but what you are really looking for is the promise of possibility. You don't know *exactly* what will happen, but you do want to make sure there is enough space for action and reaction to occur. We talked about this in Chapter 4 in relation to how much agency you want to allow your participants, and this is why it is such an important consideration. The function of story structure in a format is to decide where to apply the pressure – emotional, relational, physical, intellectual, or a mix of all four. For many of the format categories (e.g. Competitive, Perform Something or Change) you don't know how people will perform under pressure or alongside other people or what their skill levels are, but what you want to consider is what you *think* might happen. Where and what are the possibilities? Where is the potential drama? Caroline Roseman put it this way:

> Every format I develop comes with a "rulebook" – but you need to be prepared to see that rulebook ripped up once it goes into production because with anything character-led you have to have faith that your cast will provide story that the production team can be reactive to. However, these are entertainment formats, not documentaries, so always make sure you keep the format beats that guarantee drama and fall-out.

There may be challenges around relationships between contestants, around working with or alongside other contestants. In *The Apprentice* teams have to work together to win a task but they are also in competition with each other once they get to the boardroom. Are they having to work against other people? Or are they working together in some cases but are ultimately in competition with each other? Or are they working completely alone? Are they forming alliances across the competition?

The role of the presenter can be a crucial one here, and we'll talk more about casting in subsequent chapters, but in this context, the presenter is there to provide someone on-camera to elicit reactions from participants, and perhaps judges, as well as to fill in with their own reactions. In *Interior Design Masters* (DSP/Banijay, 2019–present), the presenter Alan Carr is the link between participants and judges, asking how people are, commiserating, bantering, offering and asking for opinion and responses. Many of the emotional moments are elicited by the presenter, which builds tension and emotion across the episode. This "exchange of behaviour in action/reaction", as McKee called it, is absolutely critical.

Exercise: Finding the Beat

- Pick one of the format points that you identified for your act structure, the activity, task or moment that needs to happen.
- Break it down further and get more specific. How will it work? For example, In a Make Something Competition the participants are given a task to complete. Who gives them the task? What are the parameters? Is there enough tension? What is the reaction to the news? Dismay? Anticipation? Excitement?
- *There is your first beat!* (If you think everyone will just shrug and say "ok", then time to ratchet things up a notch or six! Less time? More items? More detail? Working in teams? What will get you that reaction?)
- Now do it all again with another element in your act structure. Make the pressure of being on a show work for you. As Nell Butler says, 'it's harder to be in your own home, even if you've cooked a dish zillions of times before [but] when you have a crew there suddenly things start going a bit wrong and you forget to add the coriander'.

So far, you have identified some of the bigger format points that will form the stepping-stones of your action, and then thought about placing them into a three-act structure. Then you have thought about the smallest elements in the story, the format beats which encourage an "exchange in behaviour in action/reaction" for your characters and participants, whilst bearing in mind that we are always looking for forward momentum in the story. We don't want to feel as though it is standing still, veering off course or, worst of all, going backwards. The rest of this chapter will look at some specific moments that, depending on your idea, might help keep things moving.

Challenge It!

In any format there must be challenges to be overcome. They might be big or small, depending on your topic. *I'm a Celebrity: Get Me out of Here* (ITV

Studios, 2002–present) challenges the fear of creepy crawlies and the "mind over matter" required to eat some unusual choice item, whilst *SAS: Who Dares Wins* (Minnow Films, 2015–present) challenges the physical and mental endurance of its participants, but other formats offer gentler challenges, such as a happy memory retrieved through the repair of a treasured item, a skill to be mastered or simply recognising the need for change. Challenges can be external tasks to be completed, skills to learn, a craft to perfect, performances to complete, but they might also be internal and related to personal anxieties and lack of confidence. Relationships of all kinds can also form challenges between participants, teammates, coaches, mentors, even judges. You might want to revisit some of the hook and driver questions in Chapter 3 for inspiration.

In considering your challenges you want to consider how to stretch your participants in a meaningful way. The challenges have to fit with the inherent tension and the key driver that needs to be answered. Jonathan Meenagh refers to a "pass/fail" moment, where each scene makes it clear to the audience what the protagonist's challenge is at that point, and whether they have succeeded. Whilst Caroline Roseman described working on *Dirty Dancing: The Time of Your Life* (Living TV, 2007), pointing out the importance of distinctive challenges for the participants where the participants

> were always working towards a big dance off that would determine whether they stayed in the competition or were eliminated. However, each episode would also feature a smaller challenge in the build-up to help ramp up competition mid-way and provide additional stakes. So, you think about the running order of the show even during the development phase and ask yourself whether there are enough activity spikes and reveals throughout the entire episode to sustain your audience for the entirety – not just for the last ten minutes. But these challenges and reveals can be meaningless if they don't lead to something. Every action needs a consequence – otherwise it's redundant and probably isn't worthy of the final cut.

That chain of cause-and-effect has to make sense in terms of pulling the audience through to the finale.

So, the challenges and conflicts need a reason to be there. They are building towards your conclusion, but they should also be providing moments for the reaction inherent in the format beats. The responses need to make sense, the emotion has to be appropriate to the situation and needs to fit in with the overarching arc of the story. The combination of format points and format beats in your three-act structure is what helps to make the format sellable. They form the basis of your format bible.

Exercise: Set the Challenge/Get the Emotion

- Bearing in mind that your format needs emotional engagement from participants and buy-in from the audience, where are the challenges for your participants?

- List all the challenges that they may need to overcome. Don't worry if you write too many. You can always cut it down later. What are the external challenges (that make up your format points) and what are the internal challenges (that make up your format beats)?
- Have you set up obstacles, challenges and situations that have a clear relevance to the story?
- Have you ensured that there are places where the participants have to make a choice or decision?
- Have you left space for reactions and emotion to come through?
- How do these challenges fit in with the stepping-stones and the overall act structure above?

A High-Wire Act

You want the audience to keep watching for the whole programme. You don't want them to just tune in for the start and the finish – so what is keeping them watching throughout? A good story is not just about having everything in the right order; it is also about keeping the tension high and ensuring that there are enough unexpected moments or surprises – often called reveals – to keep an audience engaged. So, it is not enough to identify key moments, they *have* to build to a climax and each one must feel bigger than the next. Don't be afraid to think quite literally especially in the case of an obstacle course, or emotionally if it involves a change or a Competitive format that involves performance, or a physical, mental or intellectual challenge or in terms of money. In Chapter 4 we talked about the inherent tension. We have also talked about creating a cause-and-effect chain of narrative, but go back and look at the smaller moments and think why are these interesting? Are they interesting enough?

Of course, each format has its own type of tension. *The Repair Shop* with its reveal of whether the toy has been mended and the emotional reaction from the owner is on a very different level from whether someone will abseil down a cliff when they are terrified of heights in something like *SAS: Who Dares Wins*. In *The Island with Bear Grylls* (Shine TV/Banijay, 2014–present), Jonathan Meenagh explained that *every* scene had to be

> life or death because… [otherwise] you get into, "oh, you know, he's been a bit rude to me and I'm a bit annoyed about how rude they're being". If it's not life or death, then it shouldn't be in there and every scene was cut to answer the question "could you survive"?

That was the essence of the show, and it needed that kind of tension. In a show like *Strictly Come Dancing* (BBC Studios, 2004–present) as the series progresses and skills improve, it may no longer be about whether they make mistakes in their live performance, but more about can they keep building up their performances and stay out of the dance-off when everyone else is also getting better? Stakes are also higher for the audience because by then they have their favourite that they want to keep watching.

This is why it is important to establish your key driver through the story. It will help keep you focused on what really matters, stop you from being distracted by a task or obstacle that might be interesting or mildly entertaining but doesn't keep things moving.

Another way to build in tension is to layer in surprise. You can do this with twists and surprises to your format points. Caroline Roseman talked about the "secret sauce", the moments where the participants think they know what is coming but she said, 'but what they don't know is dot dot dot'. Where, for example, a competition format decides it is a double elimination this week, or there is a different guest judge, or they must work in teams, or a previous competitor is brought back, and so on. However, *Dragon's Den* (BBC Studios, 2005–present) compresses tension into each story segment of each episode and does so through the real-life entrepreneurs who come onto the show. As we've described in *Dragon's Den*, story doesn't even build across the whole episode, but each pitch is so intense it keeps the audience watching. Interest is piqued by the product, you feel for the entrepreneur as they start to lose Dragons, and they struggle to answer questions, but then they get an offer! The twist is that it isn't the offer that they wanted. This is the tension inherent in many stories – you get what you want, but not in the way you were expecting, so now what do you do? Sometimes the entrepreneur will come back and accept or make a minor adjustment and accept and everyone's happy. Sometimes they'll reject the offer knowing that they don't want to give away that much of their business and that's also acceptable, but sometimes they'll come back with a counteroffer that's just way off the mark and then they have to watch their dream crumble through their own actions. And that's why people watch. Not just to see if they get an offer, but to see what they *do* with that offer. The story isn't over when the offer is made. The final decision rests with the person who has the most emotional investment – the entrepreneur. And the audience never knows for sure which way it is going to go until it happens.

Exercise: Take the Strain

- What type of tension works for your show? Talent? Determination? Endurance? Skill? Playing the game?
- How does this tension relate to the basic shape of your story, and your driver or the core of your idea?
- How does one challenge lead to the other and do they build the tension? Are they in the right order? What happens if you change the order?
- Where can you build in twists or surprises? Where could you bring in surprise in your show? What are people expecting to happen and where could you overturn that expectation. You don't want constant surprise but enough to keep the contestants and the audience – on their toes.
- What are you building to? What's the final reveal?

The Pot of Gold

Because, of course, the biggest reveal, the biggest surprise of all has to come at the end. As Aristotle pointed out, your story shouldn't just conclude at a random point but should settle the question that has been running throughout the episode (and/or series). As always in an audio-visual medium it is good to think of a way to *show* that we have reached the end. If there is a pot of gold at the end of the rainbow, how will you show that – the top of a leader board, prizes, evictions, pairing up, a handshake. We encouraged you to "start at the end", but what does that "end" look like?

It doesn't have to be completely life-changing but as Nell Butler says, 'you have to think about what you can do to make it matter'. In the case of *Come Dine with Me*

> the prize is not life-changing, in fact it is relatively small, but you sort of understand that it works because people are house-proud, or proud of their cooking, and so you buy into the fact that it matters to them and then it matters to you.

Or as Kate Phillips put it, 'that last fifteen minutes, how do you really build it and especially in quiz and game shows, what is the build?' Consider what that final shot will be? Do you need to go back through all your story elements one more time and make sure that it's all building towards that final moment?

Formats are constructed stories which are designed to follow repeated steps. They follow a structure, a designed order of information or events, that you construct to build your story. We considered several layers of story – the three-act structure, the format points that build in action and the format beats that build in emotion – and we further considered challenges, tensions that might arise from the application of pressure at key points, from emotional, physical, relational to intellectual, providing a "promise of possibilities" of contributor responses. We also reminded you about the importance of the key driver question which takes us to the end resolution, building tension, reveals or cliff-hangers along the way; these all keep the audience engaged, anticipating and the expectation of a satisfying ending.

We would like to finish these two chapters on story with an important point. Most stories are over-designed in the beginning, but you need to prove to yourself, and others, that there is enough content there. It is easier to strip out than it is to layer things in later, so don't be surprised if your first iterations have too much in them. This is often part of the process. Much as we'd all like to go straight to the finished product, it rarely happens that way. It is a constant process of trying things out, seeing what works and exploring options. It is worth noting that this continues well into the production phase, often it is in trying things out that more options are found. The Development Circle never really stops, and in

Chapter 6 we will consider the ways in which thinking about the look and feel of the show can add yet more layers to your idea.

References

Archer, W., 1912, *Play-Making: A Manual of Craftsmanship*, Boston, Small, Maynard and Company.
Aristotle, 1987, *Aristotle Poetics*, Translated by R. Janko. Indianapolis, Hackett Publishing.
Bordwell, D., Thompson, K. & Smith, J., 2020, *Film Art: An Introduction*, 12th ed. New York, McGraw-Hill Education.
Field, S., 1982, *Screenplay: The Foundations of Screenwriting*, New York, Dell Publishing.
Horace & Persius, 2005, *Horace: Satires and Epistles. Persius: Satires*, Translated by N. Rudd. London, Penguin Classics.
McKee, R., 1997, *Story: Substance, Structure, Style and the Principles of Screenwriting*, New York, HarperCollins Publishers.
Yorke, J., 2014, *Into the Woods: A Five-Act Journey into Story*, New York, Abrams Press.

6   Design It

You know what hook or insight you are tapping into, you have considered the basic shape and key stepping-stones of the story, and you have thought about how to leave room for reaction and emotion. Now it is time to consider how your show might look and sound. This might seem simple, almost superficial, or perhaps even someone else's job, someone like a production designer, but the general look and sound of the show should not be a last-minute consideration as a "nice to have". It should be an obvious and fundamental part of how your story works and it can be the magic ingredient that really brings your show to life or adds an extra layer of tension. Ana de Moraes always asks her teams: 'what are we going to see, what are we going to see in the show'.

There are two related aspects that make the style of your show as important as the story building blocks and format points. First, working to visualise what your audience will hear and see will have the vital effect of helping to clarify the emotional accent of your idea. The visuals should be working to emphasise and underscore the emotion, the tone and the values of your show because style is something audiences are able to decode very quickly, whilst they are making a judgement about what kind of show this is going to be. The second aspect is the capacity of sound and vision to present the distinctiveness of your show and make it stand out. We said in previous chapters that there are (probably) a limited number of format types and a limited number of story shapes, but the precise way they are translated into sound and vision on the screen leaves a whole world of possibilities to make your show appear fresh and new.

So, in this chapter we will look at how to create the look, the feel and the tone of your story world and make it distinctive enough to stick in people's minds.

Exercise: Getting Your Eye In (Again)

In the introduction we asked you to look at a range of formats and make some notes about what you were seeing and hearing on screen. You can go back to those notes now, or start afresh, looking at two or three shows that sit within the same category such as the Make Something Competition formats, a People Change format or what about the All on the House Choice formats.

DOI: 10.4324/9781003050650-6

Without worrying about the story structure and format points, write out what makes them different from each other in terms of look, style and feel. Think about the pace and "energy", as well as things like colour choices, camera shots and musical styles.

Where in the World?

In Chapter 4 we introduced the concept of a story world, when we considered whether a format took place in a Real, Studio or Enclosed world as one of the early large decisions you might make about your format. But what do we mean by story world exactly? The total world of any story is sometimes called the *diegesis* which comes from the Greek meaning "to narrate" and it means the created world in which the story action takes place. In the case of a format, it means that when you design the show you set the boundaries: you decide who's allowed in and out, you ensure what rules they have to follow and how many there are and work out who is in charge. In the format paradox of "real but not real" you decide where that sliding bar will sit. Perhaps it will sit very close to the Ordinary World as in *Race Across the World* (Studio Lambert, 2019–present) which follows teams in their travels. Perhaps the story world will be a specially built Studio World where most quiz shows take place, or perhaps in a completely Enclosed World like *Love Island* (ITV Studios/Lifted Entertainment, 2015–present).

However, this is a little more than just deciding if you are in a set or on location (though we will come back to this again later) because there should always be a sense that entering a story is entering into another world, and part of the joy of being a format creator is that you get to create that world. Joseph Campbell, who explored the common myth of the Hero's Journey, described it as a venturing forth

> from the world of common day into a region of supernatural wonder: fabulous forces are there encountered, and a decisive victory is won: the hero comes back from this mysterious adventure with the power to bestow boons on his fellow man.
>
> (Campbell, 1993, p. 30)

If that sounds like the basic shape of many formats, albeit in more fantastical language, it's because it is! One of Christopher Booker's *Seven Basic Plots* (2004) is the "Voyage and Return", and some examples of this type of story are *Alice in Wonderland* (Lewis Carroll, 1865), The *Wizard of Oz* (L Frank Baum, 1900) or *The Chronicles of Narnia* (CS Lewis, 1950–1956), which are all classic children's novels adapted many times for film and television. They all involve the protagonist being whisked away – down a rabbit hole, by a tornado or through a wardrobe to another world entirely where the rules are very different to the everyday world they knew.

This idea of entering the "special world", going on a journey and leaving the "ordinary world" behind describes what happens in a format, particularly those which involve entering an enclosed world such as *Ex on the Beach* (Whizz Kid Entertainment, 2014–present) or *Love in the Flesh* (Ten66 Television, 2022), or many other dating shows, including the restaurant where couples meet in *First Dates* (Twenty Twenty/Warner Bros. Television Productions UK, 2013–present). But, as we discussed in Chapter 5, even in shows where they appear to be in the ordinary world, such as in *Hunted* (Shine TV/Banijay, 2015–present), they are still entering a special world that is separate from their everyday world, a world where they are on the run and where there are rules in place to catch them out. Remember that formats are "constructed reality" and the construction of the "special world" is an important part of their makeup. So, how "special" is your world?

At first sight those children's stories may seem very far removed from formats, as they rely more on a sense of magic or fantasy, but as we keep saying even formats that seem close to the ordinary world are heightened in some way. Richard McKerrow spoke of how *The Great British Bake Off* (Love Productions, 2010–present) evoked a sense of "magical realism". The tent is beautifully decorated, it is never untidy for long, baking magic happens, utter failures are few and far between and never a cross word is spoken. It is a special world of kindness, support and cake. Formats draw on that sense of clearly entering a place that is far removed from everyday life, or, if it is like everyday life, then it is a more heightened or concentrated version of it. Five dinner parties in a week? Bringing a fairy tale to life through a dance? Whilst these formats don't follow the exact stages of the "Voyage and Return" story, they do offer pared-back versions.

As we saw in Chapter 3, the ideas behind formats often come from the real world with real concerns but developing a format means making a "special version" of that real world, blending the ordinary world with just enough format magic to draw the audience into its "same but different" stories. You don't want to create a world that is completely unrecognisable, where you have to explain why the sun never comes up, or why the sky is green. Instead, you want to take something from the real world that we already know the rules of and then start to play with them.

Historically, fantasy and reality have been seen as binary opposites, but in fact reality in the context of artistic production is really about mimesis (meaning to imitate). In Chapter 2 we discussed a shift in western culture towards a more scientific logical view of the world, whilst artists went in the opposite direction. In the 17th century, Johannes Vermeer sought to paint external reality as accurately as he could, but by the early 19th century, Romantic painter Caspar David Friedrich was trying to depict his inner emotional world and by the early part of the 20th century Surrealists like Leonora Carrington (1917–2011) and Remedios Varo (1908–1963) were trying to paint what their unconscious looked like. This shift is relevant when thinking about contemporary "realism". Mimesis aims to imitate external reality, whilst fantasy relates to the inner world of the imagination and all artistic production (which cannot be reality itself) exists on a sliding scale: from closer to the external world of objective reality or closer to the inner world of the imagination.

So, when we say formats are "real but not real" we refer to their constructed status. They are not as close to the fantasy pole as drama, but neither are they as close to the mimetic pole as documentary. Formats are closer to the middle of that scale, but they might still fall closer to one side than the other. The tighter the format, the more constructed the world, the less agency participants have, the more fanciful it becomes.

For example, *First Dates* (Twenty Twenty/Warner Bros. Television Productions UK, 2013–present) is set in a restaurant because that's where first dates often happen. It also allows you to borrow the rules for dating/eating in a restaurant to help structure the show. It is also filmed in a real restaurant in London (Taylor, 2017), but the restaurant is completely taken over when filming is in progress and there is extra set dressing in terms of flowers on the tables, and extra lights. Everyone in that space is connected with the show, and from series three onwards the restaurant staff are also part of the cast. So, it is a special kind of restaurant, where the staff are in on the date and willing the "first daters" to succeed.

Strictly Come Dancing (BBC Studios, 2004–present) borrows from the world of ballroom dancing competitions, but most of the action happens within one large custom-built set, except for one location trip to the Blackpool Tower Ballroom, the UK home of ballroom dancing. Half the competitors are celebrities and amateur dancers at best, the couples are created by producers, and the audience can see the couples training, is given backstage access, some insight into the judges' decisions, and at the end of the story, also agency in deciding who the ultimate champion will be. This is a very special version of a ballroom dance competition.

Location, Location, Location (IWC Media, 2000–present) is filmed entirely on location, where couples face the challenge of moving house, but they have two property experts on hand who use their combined knowledge and skills to find fresh properties to view. However, the experts also act as life coaches, digging into personal histories and back stories to understand and challenge the participants assumptions and inflexibility, encouraging them towards sensible, realistic compromises. Kirstie Allsopp and Phil Spencer are specialist property finders, not estate agents, and they bring something very different to the process. It is that personal touch that makes the house-hunting world of *Location, Location, Location* special.

So, bearing in mind that if formats are, by their nature, never totally real, how "special" is your story world going to be?

Exercise: How Special Is "Special"?

Thinking about your topic and your basic story shape developed in the previous chapters, list the elements (rules, format points) that are closer to the ordinary, everyday world. Being aware of these will help you decide which ones the audience will need in order to understand your story world. Check in with your insight and driver too.

Now thinking about those everyday world elements, what could you enhance to make them more magical, more fantastical even? What is the perfect date?

How do you find your dream home? How do you win the treasure, whether that's £50,000 or a new partner or a new recipe, a new home or a Number 1 song? Let your imagination run wild (making use of the spontaneous mode of creativity), and then maybe dial it down a little again. As Richard McKerrow explained,

> yes, we ended up in a tent because it was partly the country fair thing and everything else, but it was also a practical place where we could put twelve ovens… What I'm trying to say is… it's a kind of balance between idea meets reality.

Sensible Advice

Now consider how you want your audience to feel when they watch it. The reason dating shows tend to be set on hot beaches or tropical islands rather than a wet winter city is because people are often looking for somewhere to "escape to". If your insight is tying into a feeling of escapism and romance, then you don't want your participants and audience to be overwhelmed by a feeling of gritty reality.

- What is the balance of real life and fantasy in your idea? List them out. You may be surprised to see how many rules there are in even a simple situation.
- Do you need to lean one way more than the other?
- Which ones would you want to tighten or enhance or adapt? Does it need a little more sparkle, or emotional focus?
- Start thinking about what would need to be in the set design or on location to help set up this world.

Setting the Right Tone

The story building blocks of Chapters 4 and 5 explore what action might be present in your format idea, but tone gives consideration to how the story is specifically expressed. Tone relates to the general character of the format, but it is important because from that general character an attitude can be discerned, and from that attitude, the values that imbue your programme. Every format show has a different tone. It could be gritty or glittery; argumentative or romantic; challenging or soothing.

In general terms words like "tone" and "style" are words that cover everything to do with the set design, music choices, basically anything to do with the feel and look of the show, or as Narinder Minhas puts it, what gives it "the most dominant flavour". Flavour is a great way of thinking about it because that flavour suffuses food all the way through, the way that tone should permeate through the whole show.

Whilst the tone of a show can sometimes be hard to define precisely, it is one of those things that is very obvious when it works, and equally obvious when it does not. What you really don't want is a show with no tone, that doesn't stand out and that could be interchangeable with anything else. Along with the characters, which we will come to in Chapter 7, it is tone that helps to give a show its consistency and distinctiveness. There are certain areas that get covered a lot in formats – dating, cooking, property – but each show does it in its own way. Some of that is down to structure, some of that is down to casting and some of that is down to tone, or, you'll usually find, a combination of all three. Each show feels fundamentally different to the others.

It can be hard to define tone when you are watching and so it is even harder to explain when you are developing an idea. There are ways to approach coming up with tone that involve approaching it from the side rather than head-on. When you're talking about characters or tasks or incidents, it can be easy to point to them and say – there they are! But with tone it is much harder. Things like set design and music can contribute an enormous amount to the tone of a show but you still have to decide what that tone is. A show that contains a story world that is full of danger feels and looks very different to one that is full of delight.

As with many things in development coming up with tone does not happen separately from the other parts of the show but here are some ways to get started.

Tone is about what feeling you want to evoke. In *Who Wants to Be a Millionaire* (Sony Pictures Television, 1998–present), the premise of the show is so simple (usual caveat – something that appears simple always involves a lot of work). The contestants answer a set of multiple-choice questions, asked by a host and win a million pounds. It is a simple, clear, linear story, even if you take into account the complicating factors of the "safe havens" and the lifeline options to "phone a friend" or "ask the audience", but what builds the tension and makes it so compelling is the timing, the music, the lights and the close-ups. They help to ramp up the tension as the money on offer increases. The host isn't unfriendly, but often introduces doubt asking, "are you sure" and "final answer" on the larger money questions, and thus giving great format beats for reaction from the contestant. The lights lower, the music that mimics a heartbeat kicks in and there is a camera trained on the contestant's face. The pressure is on.

Now compare this to *Pointless* (Remarkable Television, 2009–present), where there is still a possible jackpot of money to be won (although significantly lower than *Who Wants to Be a Millionaire*). Here the set is based on a circle with the teams and presenters arranged around the outside facing each other, there is more gentle humour in the interactions between presenters and contestants, and the premise itself is an inversion of the usual setup of gaining points to win. Both quiz shows work incredibly well within their own world and rules, and both are very successful formats, but, despite a similar competition premise – answer questions to win money – they have a very different tone and feel to each other.

In some situations, the risks in the real world can feel very high but you don't want the show to feel tense. For example, Gerard Costello explains that on *Location, Location, Location* if a participant is thinking,

> "I'm going to take all my money and put it into this and then I'm going to have to live in it and live with that decision for years, or for the rest of my life" then that is very high stakes – and the tone of the programme has to

balance that out so actually what we're doing is we're making this all right, we're making this feel a little lighter, happier and safer.

With Kirstie and Phil (the presenters) the buyers have expertise on their side, someone to help them make decisions based on years of experience and knowledge, and so the tone doesn't feel intense even though the participants have to make a very big decision. The show also allows for its participants to decide "not to make a decision today", and the looser nature of the format construction leaves space for this as an outcome.

Exercise: Striking the Right Note

Go back to your notes from the first exercise in this chapter and consider those shows again, but this time try to sum up the general tone of each one.

- How tense do you feel and how does anything with the design contribute to that?
- What words would you use to sum up how it looks?
- What colours are used?
- What type of music is played and at what points?
- How does it make you feel? Happy? Nostalgic? Competitive?
- Does the mood change, or does it stay the same throughout?

Once you've done this, you'll see (hopefully) that each show has different lists and then you will also see that it should be reflected in the set design and the feel of the show. *Strictly Come Dancing*'s ballroom dancing competition story world should evoke glitter and bright colours and joyful music – and that is what plays out on the screen. Whilst *Masterchef* (Banijay, 1990/2005–present) may conjure up words like precision, excellence, clean and gleaming, but these are evoked through stainless-steel cooking implements, shiny ovens and white aprons. It doesn't matter that what we often see on the screen are messy tables full of ingredients and chefs sweating as they try to complete a meal in time, because the overall feel is one of a pristine, almost professional, kitchen, striving for perfection.

Good Value(s)

When you design a world, you have to consider the values it holds dear. We do come back to the question of "values" in Chapter 8, albeit from a more personal perspective. What are the principles and standards of behaviour expected in this world? Is it a fair world? A just world? Is it an unpredictable world? Who gets to decide what matters? Who gets to decide who wins and who loses? This is a good time to go back to the insights you discovered in Chapter 3. If you decided then that your show was about confidence, or craft, or community, or whatever, then think about how you would reflect that in your show. What types of situations would take place to bring those elements out? What standards are people held to? How will you design that into the look and sound of the show?

The judges often play a leading role in this area. In *The Great British Bake Off* (Love Productions, 2010–present), Richard McKerrow pointed out that the judges' word is final because that is what they are there to do. 'The judges are the judges of the competition and that's why sometimes decisions are unpopular. Sometimes they're unpopular with the production crew, sometimes they're unpopular with the audience but they are the judges. You can't ever question the judges'.

For this competition show, they are the ones who decide on the value of what they are judging. It is their judgement alone that counts, but with other Competition formats the judges may take it so far and then it is up to the audience – either a live studio audience, as in *The Masked Singer* (Bandicoot, 2020–present) or a public vote as in the final rounds of *The Voice* (Talpa/Lifted Entertainment, 2012–present, UK version). When the public are asked to vote, they are often asked to vote for their favourite. That favouritism may be tied to a character or may be tied to who they think is doing best within the confines of that particular world and that will differ from show to show. Switching from a judging panel assessing the quality of skills on display to an audience vote shifts the criteria to a vote based (in the end) on popularity. This is a value-based decision.

The judges don't have to play that role all the time. In Other People's Lives Competition formats like *Take a Hike* (Cardiff Productions, 2021–present) or *Come Dine with Me* (ITV Studios, 2005–present), the participants swap between being the judge and the ones being judged. On *Take a Hike*, the participants score each other on the quality of the route, the picnic, views and entertainment, whilst on *Come Dine with Me* they score each course of the meal, as well as presentation and entertainment. Each person will give their reasons for the score they give their fellow competitors, and they are marking each other. It is up to the audience to decide whether those reasons or the scores are fair.

However, this isn't just about having judges on your set, and it is not just for the competitive formats. In *Dragon's Den* (BBC Studios, 2005–present) the dragons are making a judgement about what they think will make a good, viable business idea based on their experience and insight. They know how business works, they know what has a chance of being successful and they know what suits them and their portfolio of businesses, and so they make their decisions within that framework. Each of them has a slightly different take on it based on their own interests and experiences but together they are setting the framework for the decisions they are making. They exist within their own business worlds, and we get to see what is important to them from the questions they ask and the decisions they make.

Even a Change format, where there are no judges and the audience has no direct input, still embodies a set of values. In a property makeover show like *The Restoration Man* (Tiger Aspect, 2010–present), there are always value-based questions about how a restoration is carried out with George Clarke the presenter, an architect himself, articulating the tensions between sensitive, even authentic, restoration of listed buildings, which might be in danger of disintegrating entirely if left on their own, with the need to create a functioning home, and the difficulties of often unexpected and spiralling costs. George Clarke offers a friendly, though sometimes gently critical, point of view on proceedings, highlighting where compromise has been made, but leaving the audience to make up their own minds about how successful the work has been. The show highlights the complexities of this type of project rather than perhaps apportioning blame. This is a values-based choice.

Exercise: Set the Code

- Who gets to decide and make judgements? What gives them their authority? What are the values on display?
- If there is an audience vote, are they being guided by rules and values in the show or is it purely about who is their favourite? Both are valid – but in terms of you designing your show, you need to know which way works best for your show.
- What exactly are they judging?
- How obvious is that to the audience?
- Through what point of view will the audience be encouraged to view proceedings? How might the show guide the criteria?

Bringing It All Together: Mise-en-scène

So far it may seem like we haven't really talked about style and design all that much. We have talked about creating a "special world", about tone and values, but having brought these important questions into focus, it is time to think more specifically about what that looks and sounds like for your idea.

The term *mise-en-scène* is one that is now used in academic film analysis more often than in production, but it is still a useful concept for helping you to scope out the look, the style and even the feel of your idea as you develop it, especially if you are not a lighting director or production designer. Audiences are very adept at grasping a great deal of contextual information from the cues they're given by the visual and aural design of a show. In other words, they infer a lot of emotional tone from how things look and sound, long before they hear actual words or figure out what is going on in the story.

The term *mise-en-scène* originally comes from French theatre and literally means the action of "putting into the scene" and in film and other audio-visual productions it is used to describe everything that is staged for the camera. In the round that is perhaps a little too broad for us here but film academics Bordwell and Thompson helpfully break it down into four areas that are worth taking time to consider, at least in general terms. These are setting, costume and makeup, figure expression and movement (or staging) and lighting (Bordwell et al, 2020, p. 112ff).

Setting brings into focus where your action will take place and creates expectations about the story about to unfold. We already discussed this in Chapter 5, but let's go over it again from a design, rather than a story point of view. Again, at its most basic you could consider whether it should be set outside in the "real world", or inside on a purpose-built set. Though there are a great many possible variations and combinations. *Race Across the World* (Studio Lambert, 2019–present) is entirely on location, following the teams in their travels. *Big Brother* (Endemol Shine Group, 2000–2018) was filmed on a purpose-built set with a fixed rig camera setup giving the production team a huge amount of coverage and control. *Naked Attraction* (Studio Lambert, 2016–present) keeps all the main action in a simply designed interior studio set, with a short excursion to film the subsequent date in a real bar. *SAS: Who Dares Wins* (Minnow Films, 2015–present) also uses a purpose-built facility, although one on location, with elements of fixed rig cameras, alongside looser coverage of the participants when they are out on their various manoeuvres. *The Great British Bake Off* (Love Productions, 2010–present) houses all the action within and around the famous tent, which is effectively a set, although like *SAS: Who Dares Wins* is itself on location. The choice of inside or outside on a set and/or on location helps to set up the "reality" of your show. How close to the everyday world is it?

The next element identified by Bordwell and Thompson is the question of costume and makeup. You might think that formats don't have costumes in the same way as drama, which is true, but that doesn't mean this is entirely left to chance either. *Love Island* (ITV Studios/Lifted Entertainment, 2015–present) has a particular dress code based around swimwear and extraordinarily well-groomed participants, whilst *Masterchef* (Banijay, 1990/2005–present) focusses on the chef's white apron. *Bargain Hunt* (BBC Studios Factual Entertainment Productions, 2000–present) ensures contestants are wearing t-shirts or fleeces in the team colours of red or blue, whilst *The Masked Singer* (Bandicoot, 2020–present) is all about the fabulous and fantastical costumes of the celebrity contestants. In a fashion-based Change format, the shift in costume and makeup is the focus of the whole story arc.

Figure Expression and Movement (or staging) is perhaps a little less obvious than setting and costume, and yet how and when the participants are shown moving in a format does a great deal to establish the pace and energy of the show. Are they standing about talking? Or are they doing something specific? How long at any one time? Are there lots of people bustling about, or only one at a time? Are you hoping to create a high energy feel, or something a little calmer? This might have a direct effect on your overall setting of where the action takes place. This consideration might also encourage you to go back to your format points in Chapter 5. Are you getting the right level of movement and energy for the overall arc of your story? Is it all happening in the right place?

Finally, there is the question of lighting, which may again seem like a technical matter, but lighting is more than just illumination so on-screen action is visible. The quality, level and even direction of light can affect not just what people see but *how* they interpret it in emotional terms. It doesn't require specialist knowledge to consider lighting in quite broad ways that will still help with the tone, emotion and style of your show. For example, location lends itself to using mostly natural daylight, whilst studio shooting will require artificial lighting. Are the general levels of light high (high-key lighting) with very few shadows or low (low-key lighting) with more pronounced areas of darkness, in other words, is there a lot of light, or just a little, and does it vary with the tasks or action on screen? Is the light strong and hard (like the mid-day sun on a beach) or something more soft focus (a candlelit dinner for two)? It is also worth considering how this tracks across a whole episode to make sure it sits together comfortably.

Running across all four areas of consideration, here is an issue about colour choices, where you can choose to characterise your story world with a limited colour palette. *The Great British Bake Off* tent is all pastel colours, whilst *Dragon's Den* (BBC Studios, 2005–present) sticks to a palette of browns based on the brickwork and leather chairs of the set. However, even if you're not sure about a specific set of colours, you can still consider general tones and levels of colour – pastel versus primary versus sepia tones; or making use of heritage colours to evoke earlier times such as the ochre, olive and orange of classic mid-20th century design, or the deep colours favoured by the Victorians such as burgundy, bottle green and chestnut brown. You can see how quickly colour choices can create a strong image to evoke nostalgia or fun or indicate this is a serious business.

Television is an audio-visual medium, so we do also need to say a few words about sound because as has been pointed out, 'in practice considering *mise-en-scène* without also thinking about sound… may prove rather limiting' (Gibbs, 2002, p. 65). In fact, sound is often regarded as of lesser importance compared to visuals, but this is because ironically the 'virtues sound brings to the film are largely perceived and appreciated by the audience in visual terms' (Chion, 1994, p. viii), meaning sound tends to intensify and fill out the images on the screen.

You can consider what blend of sound sources you might hear. Typically, in mainstream productions, the voice is always at the centre of the mix, to provide effortless intelligibility for the audience, but whose voices will you hear and how often? Narrators, presenters, judges, experts, participants, family members or the general public? Then there is the style of music to consider, and perhaps additional sound effects. You might also consider something about the quality of the sound, that should blend with the issues of tone raised earlier. This might be in terms of relative loudness, hard or soft sounds, high or low sounds. Sound will tend to round out your story world, so can you consider sound as a way of adding additional realism, or additional fantasy to your story world?

Exercise: Detail It and Style It Out

- Take stock of the topic of your show, along with the hook, the driver and your main format points. Now consider the tone and the values of your show. Where is the best place to set the action? Is there a central location in the space that everyone pivots around? Inside or outside?
- How can you accentuate the relationship to the ordinary everyday world, or do you need to emphasise a bit of imagination and magic?

- Visualise what shapes would fit the emotional tone of your show. Is it an angular set or is everything rounded?
- If you had to give your show *one* colour, what would it be and why?
- What kind of lighting expresses the emotion best? Does it feel light and open, or dark and tense? Does this fit with your basic location, setting and story world decisions?
- How do people move and how much do they move? How many people are moving at any one time? Does that fit with the "energy" you imagine for the show? Who holds centre stage?
- What mix of sound will the audience hear: spoken word, music, effects?
- Describe the qualities of that sound: soft or hard, loud or quiet, high or low?

It's the One Where…

There is one final thing to consider before we leave the question of style and design, one thing that can make your show stand out and be memorable. Can you find the "Iconic Moment"? Can you identify the *one* thing that people will use to describe your show '…Oh yes, it's the one where…'.

This is the crucial "iconography", as Caroline Roseman put it, the thing above all others that will make it stand out. Iconography generally relates to the imagery of a programme, the pictures and images, and even sounds, associated with particular narrative worlds, but in this instance, we are thinking about that one shot, that one moment. What do you want your show to be famous for? The moment in *The Apprentice* (Mark Burnett Productions/Talkback Productions, 2005–present) where Lord Sugar says, "You're fired". With *Ex on the Beach*, Caroline explained it was 'people coming out of the water, Ursula Andress style' in reference to the famous moment where the actress's character Honey Ryder appears in the first James Bond film *Dr No* (Terence Young, 1962) wearing what became a very famous bikini. Kate Phillips, Controller of BBC Entertainment pointed out that,

> Some of the most successful formats have a very strong visual so if I showed you a red chair you'd say *The Voice*; if I showed you a big red ball, you'd say *Total Wipeout* [Initial, 2009–2012]; if I showed you a glitterball you'd say *Strictly*; so a lot of the time it's those pure visuals… that helps sell it.

Finding the right visuals and design features is as important as mapping out the format points and format beats that take you through the story. Together these are the elements that help you create a distinctive format and would earn a place in your story bible.

Exercise: The One and Only

Again, think of – or watch – various formats and list the things that come up in every episode of the show. Why do you think they are there? What do they bring to mind? What are the visual moments that take you through the show?

It is likely that some of these would be developed in production but, again, it is worth considering at as early a stage as possible, what makes your idea different and ensures it stands out. You can create a set of visual and perhaps even audio beats to go along with your format beats.

Now consider what visuals might fit your show?

- What would make it distinctive and hard to copy?
- What visuals help give a feel for that world?
- What could form the iconic moment or visual (or sound) for your show? We don't expect you to find that iconic moment immediately – if only things were that easy – but get in the habit of taking notes as you work through and you may find something when you least expect it.

Move Away from the Obvious?

Of course, you can use all this to enhance the story world that you would *expect* to find, but you can choose to find what's obvious in tone and then work against it! Think of what the type of show you would like to make normally looks and feels like and see if you want to challenge that. Narinder Minhas said about *Take a Hike* that,

> We were trying to move away from the traditional way people made walking programmes, we wanted a tone that was just funnier, that was lighter, that didn't take the walking too seriously, but seriously enough. I think the tone is absolutely critical.

So, if dancing is often about show and glitter and bright colours, how would you do it differently, and yet still remain true to the dancing world? We're not suggesting you challenge it or change things for no reason but think about what element it is you want to change and why. What would a fantasy version of *SAS: Who Dares Wins* look like? What if the military training was for Elrond's elf army? It might send your idea off in a whole new direction. What if the Survive Something format was about a zombie apocalypse? Actually, the BBC already tried that in 2015 with *I Survived a Zombie Apocalypse*, a reality game show that sadly only ran for one series.

Exercise: Change Your Tune?

- Think about how shows in your area of interest are normally made. What aspect of it would you like to change? Don't feel you have to change everything.
- Make a list of how they're normally made and then see if you can think of a different way of doing it.
- Perhaps go back to the "real but not real" paradox and the fantasy/reality spectrum, and then push the idea one way, then another.

The design of a format helps create the special world that you are inviting the audience to enter. Thinking about the right tone or flavour, the values that underpin the show will help transport the audience into your story world, that will be a blend of the familiar everyday world and something a bit extra. Together the design elements can go a long way to creating a world with a coherent style for your idea that will quickly set up audience expectations in the opening shots. The reason we devote a chapter to the design of your idea is not to tread on the toes of what might, in time, involve decisions made by the production crew in making your idea a reality, but rather in recognition of the fact these non-verbal aspects of the audio-visual medium are powerful tools that help to shape the emotional tone of your show. They should not be considered as an afterthought, but rather find a fundamental place in your development thinking.

Tone is a key part of the story you are trying to sell so the more you have thought about it, and the more specific relevant details you can add, the more you will bring your format to life for the person you're trying to sell it to. As you'll discover in Chapter 8, the more you can help a commissioner see and feel your show, the better.

Film director Guillermo del Toro said, 'I have always maintained that the difference between eye candy and eye protein is that the latter actually nourishes the storytelling values of the film: colour-coding, shape-coding, texture and light can become tools of narrative and dramatic weight' (Salisbury, 2015, p. 7). He was talking about drama, of course, but even in formats these are important tools for that fast setup and great storytelling.

In Chapter 7 we come to the important question: who lives in your story world and delivers the action?

References

Bordwell, D., Thompson, K. & Smith, J., 2020, *Film Art: An Introduction*, New York, McGraw-Hill Education.
Campbell, Joseph, 1993, *The Hero with a Thousand Faces*, London, Fontana Press.
Chion, M., 1994, *Audio-Vision: Sound on Screen*, Translated by C Gorbman. New York, Columbia University Press.
Gibbs, J., 2002, *Mise-en-Scene: Film Style and Interpretation*, New York, Columbia University Press.
Salisbury, M., 2015, *Crimson Peak: The Art of Darkness*, London, Titan Books.
Taylor, E., 2017, 10 secrets of First Dates, *Radio Times*, Retrieved May 2, 2022, from www.radiotimes.com/tv/entertainment/10-secrets-of-first-dates/

7 Populate It

By this point in the Development Circle, you have already expanded your initial insight by working on the overall shape of the story, the kind of action that will take place and even thinking about potential format beats that will pull out the reactions of your participants and build emotional arcs. You have also considered the tone and the look and sound of your story world. However, what we haven't done so far is consider just exactly who will populate your story world. This chapter will address that omission and help you to work your way around the critical issue of how to find engaging characters to bring your story world to life.

Although your story structure and design principles will probably remain more or less the same from episode to episode, or even series to series, the element that *does* change regularly is the people. The people provide the all-important "different" part of the "same but different" paradox. As Stephen Lambert put it, the key is

> to come up with something that is repeating and yet has sufficient variation in each episode or each series that you are nevertheless interested [in] and, in fact, enjoy the fact that you become familiar with the format and anticipate some of its pleasures…. [And the secret to that is] casting. Really, all these formats, these devices, are a way of telling or revealing the personalities of the characters who agree to take part in the game of playing the format.

The question of "people" also brings us back to the crux of the other format paradox we often refer to: the "real but not real" paradox. Nowhere is this paradox clearer than in the question of your characters, participants, contestants and contributors. They are real people who agree to "play the format". We have spent quite some time discussing the construction of your story world and, time and again, have drawn your attention to the ways in which your constructed story world is not the same as the ordinary everyday world. Formats are *not* documentary but rather an enhanced, altered or, at the very least, a bounded version of real life. Any story world needs inhabitants to bring it to life. You need characters.

In this chapter we will unpick the "real but not real paradox" a little further, before going on to consider the role of character in driving the story, along with

DOI: 10.4324/9781003050650-7

some casting considerations to help establish the importance of people to the "same but different" paradox.

What Is a Character?

In the world of academic analysis and screenwriting know-how, exploration of what constitutes "narrative" has far outstripped the question of what constitutes a "character", often leaving "character" as a rather taken-for-granted notion. This is because in drama (literary or screen-based) characters are often understood in a number of contradictory ways, sometimes simultaneously.

At their most basic, characters (in the contemporary era anyway) are usually understood as the construction of an author. In this sense, a fictional character is simply created from the imagination of the writer, and so a character is an artifice which exists only in words, or in sounds and images on the screen, as a literary or cinematic device. The only way to encounter such a character is through the text itself, where the author/writer has assigned a collection of traits to a usually named individual. Characters are thus 'partially indeterminate (schematic, not fully individuated) and are technically person-kinds who can be filled in (specified, concretized) in various ways and to different degrees' (Margolin, 2007, p. 68). Or as Margolin further explained, characters 'exist within story worlds, and play a role, no matter how minor, in… events told about in that narrative. Character can be succinctly defined as story world participant' (Margolin, 2007, p. 66).

This is, of course, absolutely true: a character is not a real person and *does* only exist in the text itself. However, where things get confusing is that as readers and viewers of that story, we tend to create a mental model of the character and then discuss them *as if* they were a real person. We assume that they can be spoken about, encountered and analysed in some meaningful way. In this context, the character 'can be ascribed inner states, knowledge and belief sets, attitudes, wishes, goals, plans, intentions, and dispositions' (Margolin, 1989, p. 4) just *as if* they were a fully rounded person continuously inhabiting the story world. In other words, somehow, it is as if characters continue to exist in the story world, regardless of whether someone is reading the story or not. In fact, this version of a character has been called a "non-actual individual". 'From this standpoint, character can be understood as an individual existing in some world or set of worlds, both individual and world being very close or very far from the actual world in terms of properties and regularities' (Margolin, 2007, p. 71). So, you can see that there is slippage in how characters are generally understood: they aren't real, but we (the audience) treat them as if they were.

This is all very well, but the discussion about standard fictional characters presents a problem for us. Many of the otherwise very helpful books on creating great characters hinge on ways for the writer to imagine-into-being their characters' inner states, memories, attitudes and so on. Egri Lajos (1960), for example, recommends setting out three aspects of a character: their physiology, their sociology (or place in society) and their psychology (Lajos, 1960, p. 32ff).

This is a problem for us because the people in formats are *not* actually characters… they *are* real people! They come with their own appearance, background and inner world already fully formed. That is not the job of a format creator. So "character" from a format point of view is a different sort of puzzle to be solved.

However, when discussing story and narrative earlier, we said that formats were pared down stories, and if the stories are pared down, then the characters are too (at least to some extent). In formats, we don't actually need to create fully rounded characters with complicated life histories, presenting their full unique selves, because they already exist, and yet you *are* asking them to be "story world participants". What is the balance of "real" and "not real"? To tackle this, we suggest returning to the Structuralists we first encountered in Chapter 4, as a useful way to think about these "real" characters in the "not real" story world.

Aristotle is usually considered to be the first to suggest that character was subordinate to the plot because it is by the actions of the plot that character is revealed, though by the 20th century it was (once again) Vladimir Propp who settled on plot as the way to understand the underlying structure of the folktales he was studying, understanding character not in terms of "who they are" but in terms of "what they did": a very helpful distinction when considering characters in the context of formats. Propp analysed character in terms of the *function* they played in the story, and in doing so he discovered that, despite the apparent variety in the characters and stories, there were in fact quite a limited number of "functions". He identified 31 core functions but summarised them into seven "spheres of action", which he then attached to the figures who usually performed those functions: the hero, the villain, the dispatcher, the helper, the princess or prize (this *was* 1928), the donor and the false hero.

In the middle part of the 20th century, building on Propp's insights, A.J. Greimas (1917–1992) reduced the number and functions to three pairs. He called these narrative functions "actants", meaning literally 'that which accomplishes or undergoes the action' (Makaryk, 1993, p. 505; see Greimas 1966/1983 for more). The first pair was the Subject-Object, referring to the person who is doing the action and what he/she wants to win or acquire. The second was the Sender/Receiver, referring to the person who gives a mission to the hero and the person for whose benefit this mission is accomplished (they might be the same, or it could be a more general entity like Humanity, Power or Happiness). And finally, the Helper-Opponent – referring to the support available to the subject (a magical animal) and to the obstacles he or she will have to overcome (a monster or betrayal).

It may be that some of this is starting to look a little familiar, especially if you are acquainted with Joseph Campbell's Hero's Journey. However, of course, the idea of the Hero's Journey itself was based on some of Jung's ideas about archetypes, as well as the Structuralist project exploring the underlying structures of narrative. All of these theorists were trying to understand humanity's long (perhaps even fundamental) tradition of storytelling. We all watch or listen to or read all kinds of stories as a way to understand and bring meaning to the world around us.

Jung's particular insight was to see these stories, which were retold over and over again, as extensions of the self, or workings of the psyche. Jungians tend to think that the reason storytelling in myth, legend, folk and fairy tale contain such similarities is because they present inner psychic experiences (common to all humanity) in a way we can consciously comprehend. As Jung put it 'Since all mythological figures correspond to inner psychic experiences and originally sprang from them' (Jung 1968, p. 256), we become fascinated with images and stories because we see in those portrayals and character references and aspects of the archetypes that exist in all of us. Such characters touch us at a fundamental level because they help us to encounter something about ourselves. Jung explored and gave names to some of the most common "patterns of psychic energy" or archetypal images, as he called them that appear again and again in stories from around the world. The Ego, The Shadow, The Wise Old Man, The Mother, the Anima/Animus and so on. It is thus no surprise that many of these archetypal images crop up in books either analysing narratives or books on how to create narratives. The hero is the most conscious part of the psyche, the ego. The Shadow is the thing the hero has no wish to be (the villain or opponent, the monster), the anima (the inner contrasexual other) is the princess, the Wise Old Man is the helper and so on. All of these story structures circle around the same insights, though the masculine orientation of such analyses is increasingly being queried.

The simplicity of the "format form" lends itself to simplified story shapes, akin to folk and fairy tale *and* to simplified character types, but although these repeating patterns of narrative function that we call "characters" are simple, they are also powerful on a deep level. All of which goes some way to explaining why formats have been so consistently successful. Formats are a lot like simple folktales. They tend to have the same straight-forward, linear plots that fall into recognisable shapes, and the characters too tend to fall into recognisable types. In fact, formats require the same "story world participants" who will take the story forward and enact the plot as Propp's folktales, Greimas's actants or Jung's archetypal images.

So, who or what are these actants, narrative functions or character roles that our real people are asked to inhabit and perform?

Story World Participant Roles

Everyone who takes part in a format must have a role to play in that story. They must perform a *function* to drive the narrative forward. Story has its own jargon just like every other industry, so let's start by looking at the main roles that most stories have and consider how that might play out in a format.

The Protagonist: the protagonist in a story is the main character, usually the hero or heroine. They are the one who goes on a journey, undertakes difficult tasks or challenges and/or undergoes some kind of transformation. The protagonist is usually the one who takes up most time on the screen and the one the audience pays most attention to. The purpose of the protagonist is to work their way through the challenges, all the way to the end of the story and crucially in terms of a format; the protagonist should be the one who resolves the key driver. The role of protagonist in formats is usually, though not always, undertaken by a non-professional.

In a Change format, the protagonist is the one who has undergone the change by the end, and in a Choice format, the person who is making the decision is the protagonist. The presenter or expert accompanying them on this journey might at first be taken for the protagonist because they can have such a prominent role, but they are, in fact, carrying out the role of a Companion which we will come to in a moment. We must care about the person undergoing the change in *Queer Eye* (Scout Productions, 2018–present), or running a restaurant in a business makeover show, such as *Ramsay's Kitchen Nightmares* (Granada/Optomen Television, 2004–2014) because in the end they are the one who is transformed. In the Change and Choice formats, it should be very clear who is chasing the goal: it is obvious who is making a decision about buying a house in *Location, Location, Location* (IWC Media, 2000–present). It is clear that someone is undergoing a whole life change in *Queer Eye* or who is pitching for investment in *Dragon's Den* (BBC Studios, 2005–present). The audience is also quite clear about who they are cheering for. So, whilst the presenter or expert may bring people to the show, it is the protagonist that the show must be structured around.

Sometimes, however, there can be multiple protagonists, most essentially in the Competition formats. This may result in a relatively straightforward entity, such as a team working together who can be taken, *en masse* as it were, as the protagonist. In a quiz show like *Family Fortunes* (Thames, 2020–present) the fortunes of a family, of the group, rise and fall together. (The original show began in 1980 and ran till 2002). Once their story is completed (win or lose), the show then moves onto a new family. In *Race Across the World* (Studio Lambert, 2019–present) a pair will work as a team, which of course brings its own emotional challenges. However, *Race Across the World* brings in a different issue for the idea of the protagonist because in Competition formats, you actually have multiple protagonists simultaneously chasing the same goal, all at the same time. It is, as Stephen Lambert says, similar to

> a soap-opera [where there may be] ten protagonists… and where the writers are having to work out how… the characters interplay with each other, what is the arc of each character's journey, … and what is the process of character development?

Whether it is *Love Island* (ITV Studios/Lifted Entertainment, 2015–present), *The Apprentice* (Mark Burnett Productions/Talkback Productions, 2005–present) *or SAS: Who Dares Wins* (Minnow Films, 2015–present), the participants are all on the same journey through the same world facing the same challenges, and each of them is the protagonist in their own storyline *and* simultaneously may be an ally or an antagonist to someone else at different stages of the journey.

The Make Something competitions all involve a larger group of competitors as protagonists, who are gradually whittled down to that one final winner. Each person who struggles with the given challenge is a protagonist in their own storyline whilst the group changes and reacts with every member who leaves until there is only one left. However, it is the group as a whole who resolves the key driver of "who will win", because the audience doesn't know till the end, who is *the one*. So, in a Competition format, each person is in the role of the protagonist in their own story, with their own challenges and reactions as they attempt to win. For Choice shows like *First Dates* (Twenty Twenty/Warner Bros. Television Productions UK 2013–present) or *Dragon's Den*, each character is bound by the insight or desire that brought them to the show in the first place. They want to find love, or they want investment for their business, or they want a home. It is the same desire over and over again but the different ways they go about trying to fulfil that desire is what keeps us watching.

This should be part of your design. Your job is to consider where interaction and possible conflict or support can happen (to enable emotion via the format beats we discussed in Chapter 6). Each participant brings their own experience to the challenge and so will react differently. So, in a format, you don't create the character from scratch, but you might still have quite a clear idea of the "sort of person" you might be looking for. This is also where that question of tight or loose formats is important. How much agency do you allow your participants because this will also affect the sort of person you are looking for. It is not a performance you need (as with an actor in a drama), but you do need participants who will fully, willingly and be able to "play along" with your format rules.

Exercise: Hero of the Hour?

- Think about your driving question in Chapter 4, what types of people would suit this question. Who would *want* to answer it?
- Who would feel most challenged by it? Who would thrive within it? You want a range of reactions.
- Would this question, and your basic story shape suit a single, group/team or multiple protagonists? How many?
- How much do we *really* need to know about them? How much does backstory add? (Some formats thrive on a good back-story, others, like gameshows and quiz shows, don't need much at all).

The Antagonist

Robert McKee spends some time discussing the principle of antagonism in *Story* (1997) because he argues that the 'the more powerful and complex the forces of antagonism opposing the character, the more completely realised the story and character *must* become' (McKee, 1997, p. 317). Traditionally in a story the antagonist is the person who stops the protagonist from getting what they want and is often the villain of the piece. In terms of formats, an antagonist could be other contestants (so whilst everyone is a protagonist in their own storyline, they may also an antagonist in someone else's), they might be judges, or sometimes even the experts or mentors, pushing the participants a little further than they might otherwise be willing to go.

However, the question of "the antagonist" may appear to present something of a problem for contemporary formats because there is no longer much of an appetite for setting anyone up, especially non-professional participants, as "the villain", as happened, for example, in the first series of Big Brother (Endemol Shine Group, 2000–2018) where contestant Nick Bateman was dubbed "Nasty Nick" by some of the tabloid newspapers of the day, after he was seen to be trying to manipulate the eviction nominations of his fellow contestants. The instant feedback and judgement from social media in more recent times can create an even more difficult experience for participants, and in recognition of this, from 2021, the UK's media regulator Ofcom began enforcing new duty of care guidelines, designed to protect the mental health and well-being of programme participants (see 7.15 of the Ofcom Broadcasting Code covering Fairness and Privacy).[1] As Jonathan Meenagh explained,

> you have a responsibility to people to make sure they're not hung out to dry, that their life is absolutely more than liveable, or actually made more positive by the experience they have, that they don't come out in a wreck… that [there isn't anything] they can't handle or take responsibility for themselves, [or] that is detrimental to them.

Richard McKerrow echoed this concern saying that production 'comes with responsibilities to the contributor and understanding that… [the] people that appear in programmes are being very brave and exposing themselves, and even more so now with the whole world of social media'.

However, although setting up an individual participant to be "the villain" would now be considered poor practice, this does not mean that there is *no* scope for an antagonist in your story. McKee's phrasing "the forces of antagonism" leaves a great deal of room for difficulty and adversity of all kinds, but not necessarily attached to a specific person. The quote also makes it clear that the job of the "forces of antagonism" is to insist the protagonist be better, go further and strive harder. In many format types, the central goal (be it Competition, Change or Choice) has to feel real. It has to feel like a real challenge to be accomplished, a meaningful change brought about or a choice with consequences. It may not always be the highest of stakes – baking a cake is not of global significance, but none the less, whatever the challenge, if it is too easy, if there is nothing to be overcome, then it is boring to watch. So, the "forces of antagonism" in a Make Something competition might be a time constraint, or the contestants' own lack of confidence and/or skills. The role of the judges might also be crucial, where their scepticism and doubt must be answered – an example of where a format beat (that moment for action/reaction and emotion) can be turned (even momentarily) into a force of antagonism. In a Change format, it might be a budgetary constraint where the contestants on *Interior Design Masters* (DSP/Banijay, 2019–present) are given a strict budget to stick to, or in a Person-based transformation, the limitations of imagination might be reached and a participant finds it hard to imagine where the journey will end. In a Choice format, the forces of antagonism might lie in bringing the choice itself into focus: this house or that house; date this person or that one? The decision itself *must* be made.

So, limitations of all kinds can be embraced and made to work for the story – budgetary constraints, time constraints or production constraints of any kind – as your idea transitions from its first inkling into a something that can actually be made. If viewed in the right way, these curbs can make the format better, more focused and distinct, and set up the story in a way that will allow the audience to discover if the protagonist(s) will bring out their best side or their worst.

As you can see, the "forces of antagonism" need not be entirely negative in nature. Formats often have a "feel good factor" and almost always a "happy ending", but the judges *must* have standards and values to be upheld; the audience must have opportunity to develop their own personal preferences (otherwise why would they engage with the competition or vote?); participants must face up to their own supposed limitations and transcend them. If there are no forces of antagonism, you don't have a story.

Exercise: Opposing Forces?

Again, bring to mind your driving question and the end point of your show.

- What is/are the main tasks/goals/challenges for your protagonist?
- Consider the overall tone or flavour of your show from Chapter 5, just how hard should it be for participants?
- What *external* factors might slow them down via the rules or format points?
- What *internal* factors (confidence, belief, determination) might affect your protagonist? These are helpful potential format beat moments for reaction.
- Is any element of luck involved? If so, how much?
- What external factors might stop them in their tracks and bring the show to a halt? This means you've gone too far and helps you to understand how far is far enough for your particular idea.

The Companion (Dispatcher/Helper/Mentor/Changemaker)

There is another set of related roles that we can look to for inspiration when it comes to populating the story world you have created. As well as the hero and the villain, Propp's "spheres of action" also include the roles of Dispatcher, Donor and Helper, which we have rolled into the idea of the Companion(s) to the protagonist, and in the simplified stories of the format, these are roles usually undertaken by professional talent.

The Dispatcher sends the protagonist hero out on their journey, as the presenters (not the judges) so often do in the Make Something formats when they tell the participants what the task at hand will be. The Helper offers assistance to the protagonist. In *Location, Location, Location*, the presenters Phil and Kirstie offer advice, strategic direction and sometimes quite frank guidance about the necessity of compromise along the way. In a Choice format such as *Naked Attraction* (Studio Lambert, 2016–present), presenter Anna Richardson guides the participants asking questions and encouraging them to explain the thinking behind their decisions.

As you can see, we have combined a number of ancillary roles here – ally, mentor, guide, confidante, catalyst – into the idea of a companion to the protagonist. The term "companion" was originally used fundamentally in the sense of a "travelling companion" which is what this role really achieves. The professional talent moves alongside the protagonist(s) and both witness their journey, and perhaps even assist in it, but however compelling the professional talent, however insightful their expertise or encouraging their advice or moral support, remember the protagonist is the one who resolves the driver. Thus, the Companion may have a vital role to play in setting in motion the story and in helping along the way, but in the end, they bring about change in others whilst they themselves remain the same, ready for the next episode or series and a fresh batch of participants.

Exercise: Three and Three

List out everyone you think you would need in your show, then see where they might fit into basic structure of three pairs laid out by Greimas.

- Subject/Object – who is your hero/protagonist/central character(s) and what do they want? To win? To be transformed? To make a decision? Get the jackpot?
- Sender/Receiver – who sets the ball rolling? Who sets the tasks, asks the questions or requires a choice? And who benefits from this? Often this might turn out to be the same as the Subject/protagonist, but not always. *DIY SOS: The Big Build* (company, BBC Studios Factual Entertainment Productions, 2010–present) is a transformation show which in 2010 rebooted and pivoted towards bigger projects for deserving families. The "receivers" in this case are the beneficiaries of the work rather than the instigators.
- Helper/Opponent – what support is available to your protagonist as an ally or companion, and what are the forces ranged against them: their own (likely) internal battles, and/or external challenges?

Now run through these roles all again, this time retelling the story your three-act structure from Chapter 4 making use of your new character roles. Who sets up the action; who carries out the action; who is for them, who is against them in each act; and what is the final outcome?

Format Participant Roles

We have discussed some of character functions and how these roles work in traditional storytelling, but let's circle around these roles, this time focussing more clearly on how they might look specifically for formats.

Contributors or participants – these are the people meeting the challenge, going through a change or making a choice, and they are usually the protagonists. With formats, we relate to people going through situations that we may or may not want to find ourselves in. Whether that's hanging from a helicopter, meeting your ex when you are hoping to date other people or cooking or dancing or performing some other skill under the eagle eye of expert judges, it is seeing how ordinary people react in certain situations that keep an audience gripped. There are often celebrity versions of many formats, and some, such as *Strictly Come Dancing* (BBC Studios, 2004–present), have never had members of the ordinary public as contestants, but as Nell Butler put it,

> The key thing about formats is that you're watching real people in situations that often you can imagine yourself in and you're learning how they do it and whether you would do the same thing in their situation. I think it really appeals to… the learning side of humans, because a format is basically putting someone into a situation and seeing how they get on with a few rules laid down by TV.

Exercise: Who Is Invited?

Let's circle around your protagonist(s) once again.

- List some of the specific skills, attributes (such as fitness) or talents you need to your contributors to have.
- To what level? Bear in mind that your story hinges on things being tough to the right degree, based on the driving question and the overall tone of the show, so, your contributors might be gifted amateurs with some skills, or are they completely new to your story world.
- Diversity sense-check – is your idea able to pull in interest from a potentially diverse group of participants?

Experts – these are people with a specific skill or area of knowledge. It could be an ability to fix leather goods or be a professional dancer or ice-skater or someone who knows everything about a type of antique, or how to change a tattoo. They do the deed themselves, or they teach someone else to do it. They *might* be a protagonist, like presenter and real-world car dealer, Mike Brewer in *Wheeler Dealers* (Betty/All3Media, 2003–present) but more usually they would be a Companion, often an ally, sometimes a mentor.

Judges – are often experts as well. They are often (although not always) experts in what they're judging in. They may have a lifetime's experience of cooking, or they have run their own restaurant, or they've been a professional dancer or choreographer or successful singer. Their role is to do just that: to judge. This can sometimes put them in the role of antagonist, but remember, that doesn't necessarily mean that they are negative or a villain. Craig Revel Horwood, one of the original judges on *Strictly Come Dancing* (BBC Studios, 2004–present), has at times been portrayed as a kind of villain, but his role was really that of the "brutally honest" judge who must be won over, and whose praise in fact often seems to mean the most to the contestants. Rather than personifying the villain, use the "forces of antagonism" concept to give you format beats. This is a more appropriate strategy, because negativity, especially in a "feel good format" must be handled carefully. The judges as a whole are the ones who the protagonist needs to impress in order to reach their goal.

Presenters/hosts – the presenters play the role of bringing the audience into the story, explaining any extra rules or back-story that need to be explained, talking to the people taking part to get their reactions, to encourage them or sometimes to help calm them down, or even asking the questions on a quiz show. For example, Claudia Winkleman and Tess Daly on *Strictly Come Dancing*, who talk to the celebrity participants, their professional dance partners and the judges; Evan Davis on *Dragon's Den* who acts to introduce and conclude the show, and as a narrator to bring the audience up to speed, but doesn't appear on screen with either the entrepreneurs or the Dragons themselves; or Rochelle and Marvin Humes on *The Hit List* (Tuesday's Child Scotland/BBC Scotland, 2019–present) who ask the all-important questions. They all perform slightly different functions as presenters, but, in terms of story roles, they all play the part of a Companion.

Narrator – in some shows there is no presenter present on screen, but there is a narrator. Sometimes the narrator is a key part of the show because of the distinctive tone they add through their commentary, such as Dave Lamb in *Come Dine with Me* (ITV Studios, 2005–present). Other shows include a distinctive voice as narrator, even though there are presenters or judges on screen already, such as India Fisher in *Masterchef* (Banijay, 1990/2005–present), or Shaun Dooley in *SAS: Who Dares Wins*. In these cases, the narrator provides any extra information that's needed to make sense of what's going on, but the audience are not necessarily all that aware of them. The use of a narrator in addition to or instead of on-screen characters is a stylistic decision that relates back once again to the overall tone and style of your show. Do you need a narrator, and if so, how overt do you want their presence to be? Like so many other aspects of creating a format, it all exists on a spectrum.

In many formats the "professional talent" can be an important element of continuity across episodes and series, whereas the "participants" are the ones that vary either per episode or per series. The presenter or host role is often given to key talent, someone well enough known to bring in an audience. However, whilst they may be vital to bringing an audience in, they might not be enough on their own to make an audience stay if the format itself isn't good enough. As Kate Phillips says, 'to launch a format talent is really key, but you can't rely on the talent to prop up a weak format. You need this format to be strong because if it's not it won't last'. Someone has to guide the audience and the participants through this world and can often become a vital part of the story (though, remember, this still doesn't make them the protagonist!)

Exercise: A Class Act

Think about what your key professional talent should bring to the story.

- Do you *need* a presenter? Work through the pros and cons.
- If so, what role are they playing? Are they a host, holding the fort and keeping things moving? Are there for support? To ask questions on behalf of the audience?
- Are they setting the tone, or adding to it in some way?
- Are they hosting and welcoming, presenting and explaining, or narrating? Or some combination? Where are they on the spectrum of giving information to playing a key part in providing the tone of the show?
- What kind of skills/attributes/personality will bring the story to life?
- What about your judges (if required)?
- How many people do you need to anchor your format? *Masterchef* has three core (narrator, two judges), plus semi-regular visitors in the form of food critics, former contestants and well-known chefs. *Bake Off: The Professionals* (Love Productions, 2016–present) has two judges and two presenters. *Strictly Come Dancing* has four judges and two presenters.
- How prominent are they within the format structure?

Casting

As might be becoming clear, understanding the characters who might populate your story world perhaps requires a refresher trip round previous parts of the Development Circle. Does the insight still hold when you think about finding actual people to participate? Does the goal of the driving question do the same? What about the construction and design of the story world? What kind of people fit the tone? In a fictional world created by a writer, the characters can be tailored to fit. In the "real but not real" story world of a format, are you sure you will be able to find the real people to inhabit the necessary roles to drive the story forward. This is where casting considerations can help.

One thing that became clear from all the people we spoke to was how crucial the role of casting is. If the participants are the ones who drive the format narrative forward, then there needs to be a casting strategy to get the right people. As, Caroline Roseman explained,

The greatest casts are those that represent a breadth of characters so that anyone watching feels that they have someone to identify with. Some casts are designed to target a desirable, young demographic, and they are important, but for me the greatest successes are the shows that can be enjoyed by both my six-year-old daughter and ninety-two-year-old grandfather.

Ana de Moraes concentrates the process by considering,

> what would the casting call be so… when you're going to cast this show, you're going to have to do an ad that's about this big, or to go on Facebook – what are you writing there, so who are you going to attract, who are you targeting and why would they email you to go on the show? For *First Dates* – Are you looking for love? Whatever your casting would be. Are you looking for love?

Stephen Lambert summed it up saying,

> casting is so important because [the contributors] need to be people who are a) willing to do it, b) are not going to be tongue tied having a camera pointed at them and c) they're open to going on a journey.

A good casting producer will find the right participants or the right mix of participants that can bring a format to life, but whilst the stage of bringing on board a casting producer or instructing researchers lies beyond the scope of this book, you should still think about the mix of people needed for the show at this development stage because it does have such an important role in the tone and distinctiveness of the show. As Narinder Minhas put it, one way that you can make sure it feels very different is to show diversity.

> I was keen to recognise, [for *Take a Hike* (Cardiff Productions, 2021–present)], that black and brown people don't go to the countryside in the same way that others do. So, I felt that this was something we could challenge: to make the show feel very distinct to other walking shows, by making it less white. And so, we cast the deputy mayor of Plymouth who is a Sikh in the Devon episodes, and we had a black opera singer who lives in the Highlands, in the Scotland episodes. We went out of our way to cast it very differently.

Depending on your insight, hook and driver, people may have a universal reason for taking part in a show – they may be looking for love, for a home, to challenge themselves – but each show might have a very different tone and feel that will have an effect on who might want to take part. So, the tone of the show *will* affect the casting and if you are still considering what your format might be, you could think about changing tone and see how that might affect who would want to take part and also, perhaps, the level of difficulty or challenge within the show. As with so many other aspects of creating a format, the level of background and knowledge exists on a spectrum – in this case from very minimal background to finding out about their hopes and fears and finding out how they react under stress. Characters do have to suit the show they are in. There's no point in entering *Masterchef* if you can't even boil an egg. Whereas if you're already a successful professional singer, you are less likely to want to take part in *The Voice* (Talpa/Lifted Entertainment, 2012–present, UK version) (although it is not impossible and some previously successful singers have entered the show) but they might be more willing to learn to dance or paint in a celebrity version of another format.

This might also require further thought about how tight or loose your format might be and how much agency your participants are required to display. A gameshow or quiz show perhaps doesn't need a great deal of agency because the presenter or host tends to hold the floor. It might require a certain level of skill, but not agency as such. Agency at its simplest denotes 'the ability of individuals to have some kind of transforming effect or impact on the world' (Mcnay, 2016, p. 39). In this case, the impact is on the story world of the format in question.

So, one way to work through these issues is to consider whether your three acts are primarily following a character journey or are you following a series of tasks? The rules of the constructed world of a format can leave very little room for variation based on the participants, as in *Ninja Warrior UK* (Potato, 2015–present) where the obstacle course is literally laid out for a long line of hopefuls, whilst in a quiz show like *Pointless* (Remarkable Television, 2009–present) the contestants answer questions, but other than a brief introduction, there is little background given. There can be some room for some variation according to participant reactions and abilities, such as *The Great British Sewing Bee* (Love Productions, 2013–present) where the skills and personalities of participants form part of the competition narrative running across the whole series. Finally, there can be a great deal of room for variation where things are almost entirely built around contributor reactions, such as *First Dates* (Twenty Twenty/Warner Bros. Television Productions UK, 2013–present) and the format points are minimal. For Narinder Minhas this was important when they were considering who to cast for the walking format, *Take a Hike* (Cardiff Productions, 2021–present),

> when you are thinking about casting something, it's important to think about the back stories… So could we find people who had an emotional connection to the walk, so was this the walk where their dad took them on for the first time, was this the walk where they fell in love, or they had their first kiss.

Finding Motivation

When asked about casting, Ana de Moraes replied,

> you have to ask yourselves, who are these people, who is your cast and why are they taking part – you always need a why… Those people need to have a real reason for wanting to take part in it and that's what's going to make

it work because it needs to be genuine and authentic. If you can't think of a good reason of why people would want to be in that show, even if it's a particular type of person – it doesn't need to be really broad, I'm not saying that every format needs to be for everyone… but what are you testing, what is it you're giving them a chance to do that they haven't done before or what are they trying to achieve, what is the transformation?

There's a wide range of reasons to take part in any show, but these do, to some extent, at least refer back to your original insight, your original driving question. After all, the participants or contributors are the ones tasked with answering that question, so, are there going to be people able and willing to do that?

Let's look at the three big category of stories we set out in Chapter 4 to see what/how the motivation might vary across each of them.

Competition formats: The Competition formats are about pushing the contributors to do something, and we introduced six variations on this theme. These range from seriously challenging contributors physically and emotionally in the Survive Something shows like *SAS: Who Dares Wins* or *The Island with Bear Grylls* (Shine TV/Banijay, 2014–present); to testing music or academic knowledge in a studio quiz show; to having to perform a song or dance live in front of a studio audience and millions of viewers at home in the Perform Something category; to betting on the value of an object and losing £2 on *Bargain Hunt* (BBC Studios Factual Entertainment Productions, 2000–present). What is clear here is that contributors are asked to test themselves in some way, and by the end, they will have learned something about themselves and how they operate under certain conditions of pressure. The contributors must have a competitive streak *to the right degree for the tone of the show*, but it must be there.

Change: The Change formats require participants to be willing to explore some particular aspect of themselves that is in need of change. This too can range from something relatively easy like getting a tattoo or a treasured object fixed, although there may be a back-story to both; to an untidy house being straightened up; to being willing to allow someone to dig deep into your life or business in order to improve it. This can be challenging in unexpected ways for participants, because to allow transformation to happen requires first perhaps a willingness to admit that there has been some failure and that change is needed. Consideration of the *depth* of change being asked of the participants goes to the overall tone of the show as well as its story structure. It may be something more fun like getting a house made over or it may involve overturning a fundamental aspect of your participant's way of life, or core being.

Choice: The Choice formats on the whole tend to require less back-story than the Change shows. In a sense, Choice is faster than Change, and so there are often more participants involved. In *First Dates* we are meeting an average of four different couples across an evening (or episode) as opposed to following one couple across four weeks, so the background stories we do get are very focused around their core reason for being there – dating and love. We also get little hints and stories about love and dating from the waiting staff and find out more about the participants as they chat to Fred Sirieix, the host and *maître d'hôtel* of the restaurant when they first come in, or when Merlin the bartender makes their drinks, but the key thing is that what we do get is very focused on the area of romance and how they view love. On *Dragon's Den* too we meet an average of four entrepreneurs each trying to pitch their idea and gain investment from one or more of the Dragons. *Location, Location, Location* finds a wide range of people to participate who sometimes want to, or sometimes need to move house.

You begin to see how character and story go hand in hand and thinking about the motivations that encourage people to take part help to sharpen up the focus of the story and its outcome. It can be harder to find that motivation in shows where we don't spend a lot of time with people but as Jonathan Meenagh points out, quiz shows

> do a really good job of narrative arc on a very, very fixed format. It's so simple, even on *The Chase* [ITV Studios/Potato, 2009-present]… you'll drop in Beryl from Bognor Regis, she wants to buy a new breed of dog, she's desperate to get this dog because her mother had it, and if she gets to that two grand stage she's going to get the dog, right suddenly… there's an arc through that in a really rigid programme.

Although he does also point out that 'it tends to work in studio where you've got a motivator around money and a clear outcome where someone is either going to gain or has something at stake and a very, very sharp moment'.

Exercise: What's My Motivation?

- Is the show task-led or character-led; tight or loose; how much agency do your story world participants have?
- Why would someone take part?
- What's at stake for them?
- What would make it worth it for them to take part?
- How does this fit with your driving question and plans for the final outcome?
- What kind of people would you want to take part in this – and are they individuals or groups?
- If you imagine your characters on the show, how much of an introduction will they get? What would it focus on?
- What would your casting call look like?

Characters take us on a journey as they learn new skills, struggle to show off the ones they have, bring along a cherished childhood toy for repair or try to buy a house or fall in love. They show the audience their vulnerabilities. They react with horror or with delight. They scream, shout, laugh, cry and show their emotions in a range of ways. They are the heartbeat of any story. The importance of casting was made clear by Stephen Lambert when discussing *Gogglebox* (Studio Lambert, 2013–present), a show that relies entirely on its participants (and one narrator). He said,

> The drama of many formats comes from bring people together with different values and class… The interesting thing about *Gogglebox* was realising we could create a show where people's different values and life circumstances could be mixed together without them actually physically having to be in the same space. The act of cutting against each other could give that sense of contrasting values. Actually, the interesting thing about *Gogglebox* is that the cast can have different values but nevertheless their responses can be similar. That can sometimes make you think, "oh different values doesn't mean we're all antagonistic, we can also have common ground".

Note

1 Section 7.15 of the Broadcasting Code: Fairness and Privacy, www.ofcom.org.uk/tv-radio-and-on-demand/broadcast-codes/broadcast-code/section-seven-fairness

References

Campbell, J. 1993, *Hero with a Thousand Faces*. London, Fontana Press.

Greimas, A.J., 1966/1983 *Structural Semantics: An Attempt at a Method*, Translated by D McDowell, R Schleicher & A Velie, Lincoln, University of Nebraska Press,.

Jung, C.G., 1968, *The Archetypes and the Collective Unconscious*, Hove, Routledge & Kegan Paul Ltd.

Lajos, E., 1960, *The Art of Dramatic Writing: Its Basis in the Creative Interpretation of Human Motives*, New York, Simon and Schuster.

Makaryk, I. (ed), 1993, *Encyclopedia of Contemporary Literary Theory: Approaches, Scholars, Terms*, Toronto, University of Toronto Press.

Margolin, U., 1989, Structuralist Approaches to Character in Narrative: The State of the Art, *Semiotica*, 75(1–2), pp. 1–24.

Margolin, U. 2007, Character, in D Herman (ed), *The Cambridge Companion to Narrative*, Cambridge, Cambridge University Press, pp. 66–79.

McKee, R., 1997, *Story: Substance, Structure, Style and the Principles of Screenwriting*, New York, HarperCollins Publishers.

Mcnay, L. 2016, Agency, in L. Disch & M. Hawkesworth (eds), *The Oxford Handbook of Feminist Theory*, New York, Oxford University Press, pp. 39–60.

Ofcom Broadcasting Code, n.d., Section 7.15 covering Fairness and Privacy, Retrieved May 12, 2022, from www.ofcom.org.uk/tv-radio-and-on-demand/broadcast-codes/broadcast-code/section-seven-fairness

8   Drive It

We began the book with some exploration of your own inner world in a bid to help you develop your sense of creativity, before moving on to focus on how to come up with, and then structure an idea for a format, but now we return to thinking about *you* again. An important element of working on new ideas is how to drive them forward throughout the development process and then to pitch them, with the support, inspiration and final commission of the people around you. Driving through your own insecurities, the constant rebuttals of an idea and working with teams to build and shape an idea requires the softer people skills we touched upon lightly in Chapter 3 when we discussed the importance of participation in ideas generation. In this chapter we will show you methods to harness the resilience to drive yourself forward and drive others to go with you to create the first kernel of an idea, to build and shape it, to persuade them to believe in it and finally, of course, to buy it!

Driving Yourself

In this context, resilience is one of the most important attributes to develop, and all the developers, executives and originators of well-known formats we spoke to told us the same story – to get an idea to final commission requires tenacity and resilience. When we asked Ana de Moraes about how many ideas might actually go anywhere, she joked,

> Don't ask me that. If I ever do the maths…it's really bad, it's tiny, it's like we have so many ideas… it's really, really hard… I think the last time I had to do that exercise internally, the bosses asked, how many… success rate and it's terrible, I think it's, I don't know, it's probably less than 10%… That's in a good year, it will be one in ten. But the other thing I think is that you don't let go of ideas. I think the good ones, they stick in your mind, and you bring them back again and again and you think maybe *now* you could do this if we do that.

The definition of resilience varies but it generally describes 'an ability to bounce back from adversity, frustration, and misfortune' (Lock & Janas, 2002, p. 117).

DOI: 10.4324/9781003050650-8

To stay resilient involves many aspects of your psychology and is associated with concepts of survival, recovery and thriving, all of which describe the stages a person may go through during, or after, facing adversity (O'Leary, 1998). The literature around resilience suggests a number of variables that characterize resilience including positive self-esteem, hardiness, strong coping skills, a sense of coherence, self-efficacy, optimism, strong social resources, adaptability, risk-taking, low fear of failure, determination, perseverance and a high tolerance of uncertainty (see Bonanno et al., 2004; Carver, 1998; Riley & Masten, 2005; O'Leary, 1998; Patterson, 2002; Ungar, 2004).

The fact that rejection happens so frequently, and is, in fact, a key part of the process should bring you some comfort. Nothing is ever completely wasted. As de Moraes says above, either whole ideas, or parts of them, may appear in later projects, and working your way through any process from start to finish is always useful.

Exercise: Know Your Drivers

As we mentioned in Chapter 3, working with others requires a good level of emotional awareness, a complex blend of willingness to speak up and a willingness to listen to others. Knowing what drives you is the first step to finding your voice, building resilience and also giving a voice to others even if their values are different to your own. If we know what our own values are, then we can harness them to give more meaning and purpose to our ideas and our personal drive to make our projects happen.

Look at the words in Table 8.1 where there are seven columns of words, where each word represents a value. Pick one word or value per column that you think is most important to you. Now of these seven, select a final three.

The three words you have chosen will give you a rough and ready understanding of the values that drive you. These values may drive the people you like, those you don't, which ideas you will fight for or not. It is therefore helpful to harness these to drive forward your ideas and to be aware of them when working with others too!

So, for example, if you think back to Chapter 3, consider how your values might be influencing you across the 5 Ps: Prepare, Play, Participate, Identify the Purpose and Get Picky.

- In Prepare, we are getting ready to be creative from different "starting points" such as commissioning briefs, magazines, journals, news, academic journals or life itself. It is possible that your three top values may drive you to focus on specific topics or trends that tally with them, and you might not notice or avoid incongruous starting points. For example, if "community" and "problem solving" were two of your words, then your focus might take you towards issues of sustainability and regeneration.
- In Play, if your values include "efficiency", then you might be less comfortable and have little time for playful random connections.

Table 8.1 What Are the Values That Drive You?

Column 1:	Column 2:	Column 3:	Column 4:
Accomplishment	Faith	Creativity	Collaboration
Accountability	Family	Challenge	Cooperation
Accuracy	Love of country	Autonomy	Compassion
Commitment	Honour	Change	Community
Competence	Idealism	Courage	Diversity
Competition	Justice	Curiosity	Equality
Decisiveness	Loyalty	Free will	Fairness
Efficiency	Morality	Imagination	Forgiveness
Endurance	Tradition	Independence	Friendship
Excellence	Rule of Law	Innovation	Generosity
Hard work	Responsibility	Intuition	Goodness
Order		Variety	Harmony
Perfection			Honesty
Quality of work			Openness
Tenacity			Teamwork
			Tolerance
			Trust
			Understanding

Column 5:	Column 6:	Column 7:
Living life to the full	Knowledge	Status
Love	Learning	Money
Optimism	Global view	Self-reliance
Peace (non-violence)	Problem-solving	Style and looks
Pleasure	Resourcefulness	Success
Satisfying self	Progress	
Zeal	Calm, quietude	
True to self		

Source: Linda Green, BBC Creative Leadership Programme, 2012

- In Participate, when we collaborate in an "Ideas team", as we discuss shortly, you may unconsciously include individuals who reflect your personal values, so take time to ensure a wider range of voices as part of your team.
- In Identify the Purpose, our values may influence the starting points for TEASER, the trends we notice, the worlds we want to access, the successful brands or the extremes we crave! For example, if "family" is one of your three values, then the stories you search out, the worlds, the examples of success, even the extremes may relate solely to family, but what are your assumptions about family? Be careful not to get tunnel vision, or too narrow a definition. Discover how others define family.
- In Get Picky, when selecting ideas, it is more than likely that the three values will drive choices on what makes a good or a bad idea. For example, if "innovation" is a core value, it might mean that you tend to discard ideas that are not completely new, whilst in reality the commissioner or buyer might be interested in a reversion of a format or a slight tweak!

The goal here is not to deny our values in the ideas process, but instead make sure we are consciously aware of them, so that we can harness them in the right way at the right time. This relates back to our discussion in Chapter 2 about being aware of our habitual ways of doing things, so that we don't get stuck in one point of view. Our values can help us in a positive way, by giving us greater resilience or tenacity to fight for an idea, or to engage others with genuine passion. As Richard McKerrow put it, 'If you believe in the idea, just because someone says "no", until it's been made by someone else, carry on pitching it'. Equally, knowing our values can help us be more objective and mindful of our prejudices when we prepare to be creative, in how we play and participate with others and in how we use TEASER to generate and then pick our favourite ideas.

An Ideas Team

It is important to recognize that though the lone genius *may* exist, as Narinder Minhas put it, development is more often a mix of "science and art"; being inspired by others, being in the moment and creating people's thought patterns in development. He explained,

> the first bit is the blue-sky moment and it's often about creating the right kind of conditions for that moment… you have to create a structure where that can happen, and you have to create people's thought patterns in development.

And of course, it is only when we share our ideas, inspire others to help build them, and to eventually buy them, that ideas come into being.

So how do you drive people to join your "ideas team" or to create an environment where they can help inspire, challenge and support your format idea? How do you get them to believe in your ideas, and to give you great feedback? And finally, how do you bring everything together into one coherent document or tape that you can use to inspire others to commission your work? The rest of this chapter will help you start answering these questions.

If you are just starting out, are not in the TV industry or have no contacts in the business, your ideas team can consist of friends, family or people linked to the subject of your idea. If your career is in its early stages, or even still at the aspirational stage, it is never too early to be thinking about the people in your "ideas team" or how to be a great contributor to an already existing team. If you are already working in the industry, you might already be familiar with different development roles including development producers or development executives, agents, production managers, executive producers, even members of your target audience, contributors and, of course, the buyers or commissioners. Often serendipity plays a part in deciding who these people are, but it is more effective to be deliberate in the network or "ideas team" you pick for your idea and in the environment, you set to help it grow. So, if you're not in a team right now, do you have peers or mentors that you can share ideas with or people that you can bounce ideas around with or ask for advice? And if you are in a team, how can you best contribute?

Is Your Ideas Team "Just Right"?

Narinder Minhas spoke of the need to take onboard the views of a diverse group of people. Speaking of an idea, he said,

> I think it's also what other flavours you can add to it and how can you make it feel different and distinctive… You've got to have people who're also diverse in different ways, that actually think in a different way.

In fact, the role of networks in delivering differing types of ideas has been studied. For example, Uzzi and Spiro (2005) looked at the complex web of collaborations and relationships between creative artists including producers, librettists and choreographers, for 474 Broadway musicals released between 1945 and 1989. They found that there was a "Goldilocks" relationship structure, the "just right" measure "Q", where the ideas team was diverse enough to create new ideas, a middle ground, and not too diverse where there was no common ground or too similar to produce the same old stuff. In 1950, Q was measured by them to be in its "sweet spot" with *Guys and Dolls* (Lyrics and music by Frank Loesser, 1950), and it bottomed out in the early 1970s, only rising again in the late 1970s and early 1980s with shows such as *Cats* (Lyrics by TS Eliot, Trevor Nunn and Richard Stilgoe, and Music by Andrew Lloyd-Webber, 1981)!

Exercise: Team Goldilocks

- Write down the types of people in your life or network; what are their backgrounds, cultures, hobbies, views of life, where do they live, what professions are they in, what are their beliefs, etc?
- If you were setting up an ideas team, which parts of your network are the same and which are diverse? Have you ensured a mix of people that are alike and others that are different?
- Are there any experts who would be able to give new perspectives on a starting point?
- What could you learn from speaking to your target audience?
- Who is missing? Make a list of any additional people who would add to your thinking or to shake it up; who is on your new wish list?
- Is the team now too big?

Is Your Creative Climate Right for Ideas to Flourish?

Once you have in mind who will be involved in building and shaping your idea, the next step is to think about what will get them to come up with the best ideas or solutions for your ideas. We covered the fundamentals of a creative mindset and a creative process for ideas in Chapters 2 and 3, now we want to think about how to lead them to work with you, to drive your idea forward.

Leadership can be a difficult quality to pin down, but it is worth bearing in mind that a leader is nothing without followers, and that followers have at least some ability to shape the leadership role. So, whether you are an aspirational team member, a future team leader, or someone already working professionally in this area, taking time to consider what Puccio, Murdock and Mance (2007) summarise as the idea of "organisational climate" is a helpful exercise. They use "climate" as a metaphor

> to describe how the psychological atmosphere in an organisation affects members' experiences. Much like physical climate… has an impact on people's attitudes, so does psychological climate. By psychological climate we mean a person's perceptions of the behaviours, attitudes and feelings that typify everyday life in a particular setting.
>
> (Puccio et al, 2007, p. 228)

They go on to point out that one of the key areas affected by organisational climate is creativity and building an environment that is safe, allows risk-taking and proactively promotes idea generation is vital, and we would add, making sure that the climate feels inclusive to a range of different views.

In Chapters 2 and 3 we discussed the value of developing those less accessible or natural ways of doing things, but television is such a fast-moving industry that space for ideas development as you move back and forth along the Development Circle can easily be forgotten when rushing an idea through the door, leading to a single vision or approach to an idea. Having a clear process and mindset will help, but it is important that you find new ways to create a space for humour, playfulness, living happily with ambiguity or remaining on the sidelines, to allow your ideas team to develop a new format.

Driving Others to Believe in You

If you've devised an innovative format and nothing like it has been made before, then it is likely to create some waves! People will need convincing, persuading, even gently prodding across the development process before even getting to the pitching stage. You will need to find ways to influence others to listen to the idea in the first place, to stay true to what you think the idea should be about or even to convince others to keep key elements, such as a presenter.

When getting ready to influence someone, to get them to believe in your point of view, it is important to consider what you want from the conversation. We call this your intention. Intention is important because it gives you a bit of breathing space to understand the emotions you are feeling separately from the change you would like to see happen. When we care about our ideas, we are likely to feel heavily invested in them on a personal level and this may come with us into meetings, or if we receive negative feedback. If you want to push it through, instead of focusing on those negative emotions, focus instead on what support you want from them or what you want them to love about your idea, and go in with that mindset.

Exercise: IWISHU

"IWISHU" is an acronym which can help you plan and navigate these conversations to ensure you steer clear of personal comments and emotions, remaining factual and focused on future change.

Table 8.2 IWISHU

To Consider	Description	Answer
I – Intention	Take a moment to decide what change you want to have happen. Then consider separately how this situation is making you feel and why. Check if this is 100% true?	*Change* – I want my ideas to be heard – yes 100% true. *Emotions* – I feel let down because I think they're not listening to me. Not 100% true, they are friendly and ask my opinion on ideas.
W – What happened?	Describe the behaviour/situation as completely and objectively as possible. Keep to the facts!	In the development meeting I didn't get a chance to fully explain my idea.
I – I felt… .	Make it your own, how did it feel or what did you think about the behaviour or situation? Use "I" and not "You", because "You" often puts people on the defensive and can make it feel personal, which means they may not listen to you.	I felt frustrated.
S – Specific	Specify what you would like in the future – what's the change in behaviour or outcome.	I would like a chance to share the idea fully in Friday's meeting.
H – Helpful	Specify what's good about this change? This is best expressed in a positive way, as a "carrot" or a benefit where both parties gain. Sometimes you may want to offer a "stick" but it is rarely useful and can make people defensive.	It would be great to get everyone's input and yours, so that I can work it up for you over the weekend.
U – Understanding	Be open to their response. Ask them how they might support this change. Be aware that what you perceive may not be reality; for example, they might not have noticed you had an idea you really wanted to share!	What do you think? How might we find some time for this?

For example, in this fictitious situation the development producer isn't being listened to in development sessions and is being cut off by the Head of Development. Table 8.2 shows how they could have used IWISHU to change their situation by speaking in a more proactive manner.

Driving Others to Give You Feedback

When you have spent time building and shaping your ideas, you may fear that if you share it, then others will meddle until it is no longer recognisable! However, in Chapter 3 we discussed the Four C Model, and it is interesting that there is in fact a suggested developmental path inherent in this model, meaning you can work up to more and better creativity. The key in stepping up from "mini-c" to "little-c" or from "little-c" to "Big-C" creativity is who you share your work with (see Kapoor & Kaufman, 2022). An idea can sometimes feel too precious to share with others, you might be concerned that someone will steal it, or you worry that they will completely change it. One way to share your idea is to share the initial hook, or purpose that you identified in TEASER without sharing every part of the story, to see if they are interested without giving everything away. The core premise or hook is also a great way to make sure that as you share and discuss the idea, it stays true.

Knowing "what your format is really about", what is at its heart, its purpose, helps when it comes to sharing your idea because if you know what it is about, then you can take on feedback and advice on everything that builds this and push back on anything that changes it. Therefore, before sharing your idea, have a simple and engaging way to describe its premise or hook so that you can steer people back to it when feedback moves too far from it. In Chapter 3 TEASER, we already talked about the importance of a hook as the guiding light when creating and shaping your idea, but it is equally as important in helping guide you to what to let go of, to let others change, to provide creative freedom. You want to stay open to creative feedback that improves your idea rather than convinced that your way is the only way. It is a rare format indeed that would make it from kernel of idea to commission without being changed in any way at all.

Exercise: Staying Positive

This exercise is designed to help you with feedback conversations and takes inspiration from work Linda Green and a "BBC Men's Room" Ideas Team carried out for *Top Gear* (BBC Studios Factual Entertainment Productions, 2002–present). *Top Gear* had been running as a motoring magazine programme since 1977, but it was relaunched in 2002 after this refresh. Linda Green and the team spoke with a nationally representative sample of men aged 25–45 years of age and discovered that men were taking a range of calculated risks, with one man even saying he would dare himself to close his eyes for as long as possible when driving on motorways! The hook for the relaunch and other male-skewing titles became the simple hook "to give men a rollercoaster ride". However, this did leave things potentially open to critique. So how could you frame conversations that help you get constructive criticism on a challenging idea such as this?

- *What is the central and engaging hook that describes what your idea is really about?* The refresh for Top Gear promised the energy of a rollercoaster ride.
- *What else could we do to keep adding to the idea?* Including cliff-hangers, competitions, comedy?
- *What are the issues that could form barriers?* Stunts could be dangerous!
- *Convert the issue into a question to be solved.* How to make stunts safe?
- *What are the solutions to the issues?* We follow strict health and safety rules with full risk assessments.

Driving Others to Buy Your Format: Pitching!

Once you've persuaded your ideas team, production team, development team, executive producers, etc that your idea is the one that should be pitched, it is time to pull it all together. In this section, we will cover the elements of the pitch, what normally goes into a pitch and what you might expect from different buyers, commissioners, platforms or channels. The truth is that there are no set rules to getting others to buy your idea as it depends on who your buyer is and their expectations, needs or relationship with you. As many of the developers, originators and executives have told us, winning a pitch is as much about building a trusting relationship as it is the idea itself; each meeting helps to build rapport and trust, and it is a process to get to know each other and share your thinking and your passion for your ideas.

The first thing to realise is that a pitch is rarely won on the first go! Pitching is often a long process and involves many different aspects – some of which are listed below – but even this is far from exhaustive, as every network or broadcaster, and each commissioner within them, will have their own way of working. Conversation and relationships are crucial but none of that matters if you don't have a good idea and a way of expressing it. Therefore, we will focus primarily on different ways of sharing your idea and getting the story across and how to bring together all the elements that we have talked about in this book. We will also briefly mention some of the other elements that start to come into play by this stage, such as budget.

Before we get into how to communicate the idea, let's address a question that is often asked – how many ideas should you go in with? As always there's no one answer but the general consensus is – not too many. Ana de Moraes thinks it's about highlighting 'the one thing that I really love at the moment, maybe two, at most three, not like here are eight top lines. It's like "these are the things we really love; this is why we want to make it"'. This was echoed by other people we spoke to. It is better to take in one or two carefully thought through projects that you are passionate about than to take in a long list of ones that are only half developed, and that you could take or leave.

Commissioners are looking for good programme ideas. They get pitched hundreds a week so what is going to help yours stand out? As Stephen Lambert put it, 'the marketplace is enormous, and it means that you are better placed really working out what your show is rather than going in with a half-baked idea'.

Of course, if you've already taken your idea through all the questions in this book, there will be nothing half-baked about it!

Different Forms of Pitches

Again, there are no set rules. A pitch can take the form of an email, a sizzle reel (a mini-advert for your show), a pitch deck (such as a slide presentation) or a document. Here we'll take you through some of the key things that it would be helpful to include but all the industry experts said that it changes from show to show, from broadcaster to streamer, from commissioner to commissioner. It can also depend on whether you are pitching for the first time or if you are part of a team with an amazing track record.

You may not be asked for any of these at a first meeting – as we keep pointing out, it is a continual process, but here we suggest some of the common ways you may be asked to pitch, bearing in mind that depending on your relationship with the commissioner (i.e. whether you've worked with them before) you may be asked for more or less.

Pitch deck – this is often done as a set of slides in a presentation and is highly visual. It is a mix of text and visuals with each section addressing a key aspect of the idea. These could include an overview of the idea, a breakdown of who is in it, a description of the set or story world, episode overviews, key filming styles, key crew and budget. Ana de Moraes suggests what you would include:

> Different broadcasters like different styles but as a rule I try to keep text to a minimum, just trying to be really concise and telling the "this is the idea and this is how it works", steps one, two, three, four, you know it's the breakdown really explaining what you're going to see in an episode. And then… most of our proposals have at the end a slide where we say why we love it so, explaining *why* we love, this is why we think people will talk about it, this is why we think you should commission it.

What else can you do to help it stand out? Ana suggests that "graphics" is a good skill to have because 'if you're not able to do a sizzle reel then you can do a really good deck that's really visual. That can go a really long way to selling the tone and the feel'. As she says you can use slides to 'show a little bit of what it's going to look like and bring humour to it if it's a show that has humour in it or make it glossy and sexy if it's glossy and sexy'. The tone we discussed in Chapter 6 should be consistently visible in the design of the slides.

Written treatment – a treatment is the written form and can vary from a single paragraph to multiple pages. It contains the same type of information as the pitch deck but relies more on text so you would have to craft words to give that same sense of tone as the graphics offer in a pitch deck. You can, of course, put graphics in a text document.

Being able to write a version of your idea is, as Narinder Minhas says, 'a real craft'. It takes real skill to bring a programme to life using just words, but often that may be all you have. So, take the time to shape what it is that you really mean. Focus on clarity and layer in the tone of the show. Graphics often do the work of that in a pitch deck or sizzle reel. In Stephen Lambert's written development documents, he highlighted the importance of bringing the story to life and what the audience will be following, saying

> the buyer needs to be clear about what the whole thing's about and why the audience might find it appealing, and then you have to explain what the central dynamic is that's going to create change and drama and conflict and humour.

A *sizzle reel* – sometimes referred to as a "sizzle" or a "taster tape" is a mini advert for your show. Narinder Minhas says 'it's the closest telly gets to the advertising industry. It's basically a commercial that you're putting together'. It will give a flavour of character, world and tone very quickly. You might use it on its own as a prelude to discussion or alongside a treatment or pitch deck. 'Commissioners love nothing more than a great piece of tape' says Caroline Roseman although she goes on to say, 'The thing with a great piece of tape though is if you really want to blow someone's socks off that can be weeks of work'. There are different types as Narinder Minhas explains,

> There are those that absolutely explain the nuts and bolts that we're talking about or give a good idea of how the show might work, and then there are just what I call mood sizzles that create an atmosphere, create a sense of what it is, give you the big picture but without drilling down into the beats.

Pitch Content – Bringing It Together and Keeping It Simple

Whether you condense your pitch into a paragraph or turn it into a sizzle having worked your way through all the areas in this book will give you a lot of material to choose from. Even if they don't all make their way into a pitch, they will be crucial for the follow-up questions that you'll get if the commissioner is interested in your idea or to have a conversation about the possibilities. By now, you should know your idea inside and out.

A *one-liner or short description* – One of the first steps is to condense the format into a short description, or as Richard McKerrow put it more forthrightly, 'if you can't describe it in 30 seconds, I don't think it'll really work'. It's a good discipline to develop. If you struggle to describe the show concisely, it suggests that something isn't clear enough and another trip around the Development Circle might be in order.

What makes it different and why now? – Tied to this one-liner or short description should be a feeling of importance, right here and right now. The inspiration and relevance of *Hunted* (Shine TV/Banijay, 2015–present) centered around discussions at the time that the UK had one of the highest level of camera surveillance anywhere in the world. Jonathan Meenagh pointed out that

> every Factual Entertainment show needs a good question at its heart that's relevant for right now and *Hunted*'s was… very relevant because at the time there was a lot about the cameras… and actually if we did have to go up against the state, could we manage?

It's also important to consider what makes your idea different because, as we've frequently pointed out, shows can have similar shape, so what makes yours fresh? What makes yours stand out? Talking about property shows which he says is a "crowded field", Gerard Costello says he is often asked for 'just that little kernel, that thing that makes me feel that I should commission this, as opposed to feeling that I've seen it before'.

What's the show about and what happens? – Once the hook has been explained through the one-liner, the time may come to explain in more detail what actually happens in the show, but even here, the emotion should be front and centre. It cannot just be a list of "this happens, then this happens, then this happens". Go back to Chapter 5 and consider the "cause and effect" narrative chain of your format points, all the while keeping the emotional pull in clear view. Is every task or exchange working to tell the story? To help with this, Caroline Roseman advises,

> to write an episode example, or even an entire series of episode examples, because it's foolproof and it's a common ask from the broadcasters before they agree to buy the show. It's a long process but can also be a very useful exercise as it forces you to get into the detail. How many contestants? Where are they living? What are they doing? What moments are going to encourage storyline and drama? How does each episode end? If it's a competition show, what are the challenges that are ultimately whittling them down towards that big prize? If it's a dating show, what are the beats that are going to bring people together but also pull people apart? Think about your audience. What world are you inviting them into? How do you want them to feel? Are you providing a balance of joy and tension that encourages them to invest? Anything that stirs the emotions is vital. I'd rather have viewers shouting at the TV in frustration than looking at their phone. You've got to make people care.

What's the tone? – In Chapter 6 we spent some time discussing tone, so circle back to the Striking the Right Note exercise and see what you highlighted around tone and your story world and how you could best show or explain that in the pitch. Tone is often one of the most notoriously difficult things to get across so spend time really thinking about the best way to help someone else feel it. Tone often has a nebulous quality, but it is a vital part of how your show will feel to the audience, so your pitch must encapsulate that tone in a tangible (audio-visual) way.

Who is in the show and why? – Of course, Chapter 7 went over your participants in some detail. As Stephen Lambert says, in a format, 'people have to be open to go on a journey that will lead to change'. Change requires agents of change, such as judges, contestants, experts, presenters or narrators and roles to play, such as protagonists, companions (allies and mentors) or antagonists, whilst on-screen talent also helps set a tone, and is a recognizable pull to target audiences, acting as a needed guide. This is a chance to explain who is in the format and why.

Who is the target audience? – Commissioners want to see that you understand their audience, that you have created a format that you know will appeal to them and have them hooked episode after episode. The idea of an audience crops up a lot in this book, after all, a television programme is something that you want people to watch and hopefully enjoy over and over again. But how are you imagining that audience? How do they imagine themselves? A modern television audience (whether linear broadcast or streamed or viewed online) is a complex composite entity.

> An audience can… be defined in different and overlapping ways: by place (as in the case of local media); by people (as when a medium is characterised by an appeal to a certain age group, gender, political belief, or income category); by the particular type of medium or channel involved (technology and organisation combined); by the content of its messages (genres, subject matter, styles); by time (as when one speaks of the "daytime" or the "prime-time" audience, or an audience that is fleeting and short term compared to one that endures).
>
> (McQuail, 1997, p. 2)

As you can see there are a great number of ways to understand and categorise, an audience packed into that one explanation, which is why we have at times referred to "audiences" plural, but it is worth thinking through them all at least a little.

Common categories of segmentation are geographic, demographic, behavioural and psychographic. Geographic naturally considers where the audience members are physically situated. A screen-based audience is one distributed in space and increasingly in time (unlike a theatre audience, for example, who have to be all in one place at one time in order to see the performance), but even considering if your audience is local, national or international can be helpful, and probably important to your commissioner or buyer. Demographic considerations usually include things like age and sex, or socioeconomic status, for example. Behavioural factors relate to audience habits, so some consideration of what devices are likely to be used for viewing may be relevant, where mobile phone viewing means a smaller screen and often a shorter attention span, for example. This may affect how you structure your episodes or how the design works. Psychographic considerations are another way of characterising an audience based on interests or lifestyle. Age may be irrelevant, for example, if you are looking to engage dog lovers of all ages in something like the heartwarming human and dog matching show, *The Dog House* (Five Mile Films, 2019–present). Remember that in Chapter 2, we suggested that one place to start looking for ideas was exploring the interests and concerns of potential audiences.

It is important to reiterate that commissioners tend to have a very clear picture of who their audience is, and you may need to stay flexible in terms of adapting story emphasis, tone or style to more directly suit a target audience. However, at the same time, developing a good sense of channel identities and target audiences means you won't waste time trying to pitch an idea to the wrong commissioner.

When your idea hits the spot for the audience, they love to play along with the format, as Gerard Costello, Executive Producer of *Location, Location, Location* (IWC Media, 2000–present), explained when talking about why people watch it, saying

> The people who are watching could say "I might choose to live there", or tangential things like "I wouldn't mind doing that in my own home", or "I can't believe how far your money goes in that area" or even "I would never pay that amount on a home". Fundamentally, people get to play along slightly.

What makes it unique? Why only us? Why you love it? – When we buy something, we want it to be exclusive, a hidden gem that nobody else has spotted and commissioners are no different. It is important to highlight anything that makes your format unique and why only you can make it. It might be unique access? Or it might be your proven track record? Or it might be a personal story or an insight about life that only you have? Passion for the idea matters. All of the people we spoke to were passionate about their idea. As Ana de Moraes says,

> I try to only pitch things that we really love… I mean, you get a meeting, some people go in with lots and lots of ideas. I don't think that works. I think you need to go, "here's the one thing that I really love at the moment".

What are the benefits to the buyer? – Commissioners are buyers who know their channel audiences and need to meet the needs of their organisations or businesses; so, as Kate Philips says,

> I think a good tip is to say to people,… if they're coming in to me to do entertainment BBC1 Saturday nights, look at what has gone before, look at what's worked and what hasn't and basically, you're coming in there thinking, "Right Kate, what are your challenges at the moment, what are your issues and how can I help you overcome them".

Other needs might include particular budget constraints, quotas on regional spend, ensuring diversity on and off screen, accessibility and talent development and many more. Understanding your buyer's needs and pulling out what makes your format deliver to these is ever more important, so don't forget to demonstrate why the format will work for them and their platform or channel!

Exercise: Pitching Checklist

As you can see, by the time you get to the point of pitching, you will have to have travelled around the Development Circle at least once, at the same time, preparing for a pitch can also show you where there might still be some work to be done. Figure 8.1 is a checklist for a pitch linked to the chapters we have covered.

A one-liner or short description	Why audiences will want to watch this format and how will they watch? Practice summing it up in one line or one paragraph.
What is it really about and why now?	Chapter 3: TEASER and Chapter 4: Shape It – What is the reason why the audience will care about this show, what's it really about? Why will audiences relate to it?
What is the show about and what happens?	Chapter 5: Build It – Is it a Competition, Change or Choice format? Or is it something new? What's the beginning, middle and the end of our story?
What is the tone?	Chapter 6: Design It – What's the world you are inviting the audience and the buyer to enter, how can you bring it to life?
Who is in the show and why?	Chapter 7: Populate It – Judges, contestants, experts, presenters or narrators. What are their roles? Why them?
Who is the target audience?	The commissioning brief – Chapter 3: Do Creative, and this chapter – What do you know about the commissioners' target audience and what evidence do you have that this format will draw them in?
What makes it unique? Why us? Why do we love it?	All Chapters! Where has this idea come from? What makes it special and why can only you make it happen? Why do you love it?
What are the benefits to the buyer?	Do your homework on who you are pitching to. What are their channel or platform needs? It could be retaining an audience, reaching an under-served audience, regional, talent or marketing needs.

Figure 8.1 Pitching Checklist

Further Pitch Elements and Expectations

Full episode breakdowns – As we mentioned before, it depends on who you are pitching to and what their requirements are. The SVOD (Subscription Video on Demand) services such as Netflix, Disney+, and other streamers, and online platforms such as Facebook and Youtube, seem more likely to expect a full pitch deck and may request a full series breakdown, sometimes with additional development funding. As Caroline Roseman explained:

> For our series with Amazon Prime Video, *The One That Got Away* (Fulwell 73, forthcoming 2022) the opportunity to make a ten-part series with one of

the biggest streamers in the world made it worth over-delivering during the development phase. As well as the usual funded development deliverables we wrote a ten-episode series arc breakdown, character biographies for our dream cast, included set designs, information on additive technology. We wanted to paint them a picture of our dream show and our passion for the project jumped out of every page.

Team – Commissioners buy from people they trust, and who they know can deliver. It helps to provide details of the originator and why only you can make this show and why you love it, who will be executive producer on it and what they have done before, casting directors and production managers too and why they are right for the job. This is especially key if you haven't made anything like this before. An experienced team will help back up your offer.

Order and endings – In terms of the order, you need to decide what to lead with. What do you think is your best-selling point? Think back to Chapter 3 and your original hook? Is that the most relevant opening for your pitch? Or is it the team making it? Or is it about serving a particular pre-existing fan base for your professional talent? Your commissioner will know their audience. You should know your commissioner as well as possible, through what others have told you, from visiting the channel websites, through interviews they may have given or even in press articles. Thinking ahead for marketing, especially for subscription services and streamers can be helpful. After all, your format will be their marketing splash, a means to keep audiences paying their subscriptions, connecting with their platform or growing new audiences.

Whether you are pitching verbally or in a written form we would always suggest having a memorable finish. Whilst openings are key to every story as their job is to grab people's attention, it is how you leave people that also really matters – finish with a flourish.

Budgets – You will need to be aware of budgets, as Stephen Lambert put it, you may have all the elements of a great idea, but 'can it all be captured and made within the constraints of a budget?' Just as commissioners have a clear idea of their audience, they also have a clear idea of how much money they have to spend acquiring content. Budget considerations may mean another trip around the Development Circle as you figure out who you are pitching to, and your level of ambition in terms of the tone, approach and story structure of your format. All these choices have cost implications. Different buyers have different production budgets; therefore, it is important to be realistic and pitch within their means. For example, multiple filming locations or billing top-level professional talent have higher cost implications, as do fixed rigging or beautiful studio sets. Take a moment to consider if these are really needed to deliver the central hook of your idea, and if so, can your buyer afford these or are you offering more than you need to meet your own creative ambitions? Buyers invariably will ask you to reduce costs and prove value for money, so have a Plan B ready that will cut costs whilst still delivering your idea and putting as much value on the screen.

So possible considerations might be, if you are pitching your idea to Channel 5, for example, how can you return to the Development Circle to bring down production costs; whereas if you're pitching for a BBC1 primetime slot, then how can you prove value for money whilst putting as much of the budget as possible up on the screen; and if you are pitching to Netflix, Disney+ or Apple TV+, then how can you make the idea as big as possible, as cinematic and eye-catching?

Over the years marketing has taken a much greater role in decision-making. This is especially true for the SVODs and streamers, who are like a gym membership, and need to keep an eye on audience churn, which demands a constant diet of marketing worthy, stand-out content that can appeal especially to younger audiences. As public service and domestic channels continue to have their budgets squeezed, knowing the needs of large US SVODs and streamers will become ever more important as they increasingly dominate the market and production spend, and become key to commissioning opportunities. Also, it is likely that the trend for domestic channels to request co-production deals or additional production funding from branded product placement will increase; having a marketing mindset, knowing your target audience and the products they use will be a skill worth having.

Keep talking – Finally, remember pitching is not a one-time event. Even if it is a commissioner you've worked with before, and you are someone with a track record in creating great content, there may still be many meetings involved. It is important to stay open to different views, whilst staying true to your hook or original insight.

In this chapter we have focused on the "people" side of developing your idea, but by now you probably realise that every new aspect introduced to the development process means another trip around the Development Circle. We began with a consideration of your own internal world as a source of creativity, but there is no doubt that you are also the driving force for your idea in the external world too. Keep talking, keep going, keep harnessing your own drivers to motivate you to believe in yourself and your ideas, and drive others to believe in you too. Be assertive when responding to others' behaviours to stand up for your ideas, whilst also respecting their views. Remember that what we perceive may not be the other person's reality.

We have also covered some of the things to think about in working with other people in an ideas team. We discussed some of the benefits of brainstorming in Chapter 3, but there is no doubt that all ideas benefit from a mix of people at all stages of development; a team with enough diversity to shake the idea up and similarity to help build the idea is a must. Build a "Goldilocks – just right", ideas team around you and your idea. When working with others, set a creative environment with room for playfulness, asking questions, being open to different views and supporting calculated risks. Driving good feedback for your idea is also an important skill to develop. Share a simple, engaging hook or premise of your idea as a guiding light for building it and a way to let go of elements that could be changed. Be deliberate in asking for positive feedback first, before working with issues and finding solutions.

The aim is always to get your idea in front of others who are in a position to buy it and the form of the pitch will depend on their preferences. However, it is worth seeing a pitch as one step in an ongoing process and conversation, with no set rules on what is right or wrong or how long the commissioning process will take. They can take many different forms. The usual ones are a presentation deck, a written treatment, a sizzle reel or a verbal pitch. The verbal pitch may include different ingredients, though simplicity and why you love it, your passion is key; the order of the pitch ingredients and number of ideas will vary but need to be delivered in terms of the needs of your commissioner or buyer. As the pitch conversation progresses, be prepared to give a full episode breakdown, budgetary details, the team and much more information besides!

References

Bonanno, G.A. et al, 2004, The Importance of Being Flexible: The Ability to Both Enhance and Suppress Emotional Expression Predicts Long-Term Adjustment, *Psychological Science*, 15(7), pp. 482–487.

Carver, C.S.,1998, Resilience and Thriving: Issues, Models and Linkages, *Journal of Social Issues*, 54(2), pp. 245–266.

Kapoor, H. & Kaufman, J. 2022, Basic Concepts of Creativity, in S Russ, J Hoffman & J Kaufman (eds), *The Cambridge Handbook of Lifespan Development of Creativity*, Cambridge, Cambridge University Press, pp. 5–19.

Lock, R.H. & Janas, M. (2002) 'Build Resiliency', *Intervention in School and Clinic*, 38(2), pp. 117–121.

McQuail, D., 1997, *Audience Analysis*, London, SAGE Publications.

O'Leary, V.E., 1998, Strength in the Face of Adversity: Individual and Social Thriving, *Journal of Social Issues*, 54, pp. 425–446.

Patterson, J.M., 2002, Understanding Family Resilience, *The Journal of Clinical Psychology*, 58(3), pp.233–246.

Puccio, G., Murdock, M. & Mance, M., 2007, *Creative Leadership: Skills That Drive Change*, London, SAGE Publications

Riley, J.R. & Masten, A.S., 2005, Resilience in Context, in RD Peters, B Leadbeater & RJ McMahon (eds) *Resilience in Children, Families, and Communities*, Boston, Springer.

Ungar, M., 2004, A Constructionist Discourse on Resilience: Multiple Contexts, Multiple Realities among At-Risk Children and Youth, *Youth & Society*, 35(3), pp. 341–365.

Uzzi, B. & Spiro, J., 2005, Collaboration and Creativity: The Small World Problem, *American Journal of Sociology*, 111(2), pp. 447–504.

9 Get Out There!

We asked all our interviewees to try to put a number on how many ideas they had versus how many ideas went anywhere. It wasn't a popular question, but we asked it because we wanted to quantify just how hard it is to come up with an idea worth developing. We touched on this briefly in Chapter 8 in relation to resilience. It's fair to say that the question elicited a shake of the head or hands over the eyes and a percentage that was pretty low. And that's from people who are successful in the industry. The reason the number is so low is because there are so many great teams out there all pitching ideas and a limited number of slots, and the process of balancing out all the ingredients of a format into a tasty recipe is difficult. But like anything in life, and particularly in anything creative, it is the process that brings success. It is persistence and talent and a great team and a little bit of luck and timing.

But this is not a numbers game. Yes, if you work in a development team, there will be an expectation around getting a certain number of shows commissioned, but it is also about mindset. Development is tough because rejection is more common than success. That's why many people we spoke to suggested working in production as a break from development. This not only helps you see what is needed for something to work on the screen but also means you get to see a finished product.

Resilience is vital in ideas development. This is true in any creative discipline and format development is no different. People work in this area because they love it, but whilst they may hope for instant success, they also know that it is a long-term process. This is a business. They build relationships. They work on ideas. They pitch them and then come back to work on them again. Some ideas they shelve for years and then they bring them back out again when the time feels right. Some, many, most, will never get made, but every so often one will be accepted and make it on to the screen and an audience will fall in love with it.

And then the process starts all over again.

The Development Circle – Let's Go Round Again

We introduced you to the Development Circle at the start of this book and, hopefully, by now you have worked your way around it at least once. We have

DOI: 10.4324/9781003050650-9

said it many times throughout the book, and we will never tire of saying it – development is not a linear process. Every time you move on to a new aspect, something else will change and you will have to go back and check, re-evaluate and perhaps make yet more changes. You will make your own journey through the Development Circle. It won't even be the same every time: every show, every idea, every new story brings its own unique problems. So sometimes you whizz round it and other times you'll ping back and forth as though you're stuck in a pinball machine.

We started the Development Circle with a discussion on the importance of creativity – getting into a creative mindset by getting to know your own inner psychological ecosystem, recognising habits of thought and finding lesser used pathways, so that you can be flexible, switching easily between the deliberate mode and the spontaneous mode and practising it at every stage. A format won't happen without a great idea, so this is the stage where you want to spend a lot of time. Don't just rush into the first idea that you have. Even if you do end up working with that first idea, you want to be sure you have tested it and made it the best it can be. Working through the creative processes in Chapter 3 can help you knock off the corners and find the obvious flaws, before with any luck spotting the pot of gold at the centre of the idea.

We then looked at all the elements that help shape a format and how similar they are to stories. As with drama, there are certain key shapes that they fit into. For us, that took the form of Competition, Change and Choice. These shapes, however, are not a shortcut or a licence to create a formula. Instead, they enhance potential great ideas by giving a constraint to work in that will allow creativity to flourish. If you are following a simple shape, then you have even more freedom to design the elements to make them distinctive and engaging.

There were also initial questions around whether your show followed a series arc or was composed of stand-alone episodes; what kind of world it took place in and what it was really exploring. Again, don't feel you have to stick to your first decision around these. Take the time to explore what your idea might look like if you changed any one of these elements. Don't settle, *really* work through those options and alternatives.

The next stage of the development cycle was to build it – to consider the stepping-stones, the format points and beats, the tasks, reveals and rewards – all the things that would happen in your show, that helped make it visual. These are also the elements that form the repeatable part of the format, that are created week after week and watched season after season.

The design element came next, and this is where, as always with the cycle, you could see how you would move back and forwards because the design is tied to the elements as well as to the decisions you made about the initial shape of your format. But this stage focussed more on what the show would look and feel like – what kind of tone you are planning, what the "iconography" might be, that stand-out visual (or sound) that people would remember or associate with the show.

Towards the end of looking at the story, elements came the sections on who would take part in the show. People are at the very heart of these shows – without willing participants the shows cannot happen. We asked you to consider first the roles that had to be carried out, before moving on to considering more specifically who would suit your show and, crucially, why they might want to take part. The real people who "play along" with your format rules are what stops the repeatable part of a format from becoming boring or formulaic. This is also the time to consider what key professional talent you would like to have attached to the project, or even to build it around.

And finally, there is no point in having a good idea if you don't know how to share it or express it well. This falls at the end of the Development Circle but there is no reason that it could not also be the start, where an idea might develop from an initial chat around a commissioning brief. It could be a conversation or a great one-liner that sends you off to build a new idea and fill in all the elements. This section also explored the importance of good relationships and how, like the Development Circle itself, relationships are perpetually in motion. There is never just one discussion.

The only thing that is true about the Development Circle is that by the time you have a polished format idea you will have gone through all the stages. The order or how many times you have done so doesn't matter. What does matter is that all these elements need to be asked and answered in order to have a fully developed idea.

The Development Circle is a tool, not a rigidly defined formula. It is up to you to use it in a way that suits you, your team or your company.

As Gerard Costello said,

> when a format is absolutely refined, when it's at its best and you've seen an episode of it, you should walk into a room and know in a few seconds whereabouts in the show you are because the format makes that clear.

Produce It

As you get closer and closer to a workable and makeable idea, the questions will start to shift more decisively from "what" to "how". Earlier in the process, keeping production at the back of your mind can be helpful. For example, considering the question of the "filming device" might help to clarify the structure, setting and design of the show. Or where thinking about the "story shape" of a Competition format in an Enclosed World implies quite a lot about how the show might look and how content can be captured.

However, if your idea stood up well to a robust development process, there will come a time when you need to work round the Development Circle once more with sharper eye on the production side of things. Does the idea in its current form mean you're looking at 12 camera crews working around the clock? Is the budget going to be astronomical (at least in comparison to its potential audience)? What about Health and Safety? If you need a certain level of fitness, have you thought about how it might affect your casting call and potential knock-on effects for diversity? As we discussed in Chapter 7, there is a growing requirement in the television industry to expand Duty of Care to the mental well-being of cast and crew as well as their physical safety. What are the risks inherent in your idea as it currently stands? How will you look after your participants on the road or stuck in one house together? What about the dangers of exposing potentially vulnerable people to harsh social media criticism?

It is wise to stay in a development state of mind, but the closer to production you come, the more you are likely to move into the deliberate mode and away from the spontaneous mode of creativity, but remember the key to true creativity is the ability to switch between those modes as required, because the Development Circle rolls on until the show is in the can and has been broadcast… and then you start again with Series 2.

Once again, we'd also like to emphasise that we have focussed primarily on television formats (in its widest sense, including SVODs and other streaming services), particularly those with a UK focus, but we know there are lots of exciting things happening out there on YouTube and other platforms. If you work in any of those areas, or want to, we hope you will take the skills and stages mentioned here and use them to make a format for the area you work in. The principles remain the same, even if the medium changes. Be creative. Find a shape. Build the steps. Design a world. And then fill it with people.

What Next?

We've shown you the elements of most successful formats today, and we don't believe they will be going away any time soon, but there's always room for innovation and surprise. So, take these as a basis and consider what will happen next? What still needs to be seen? Explored? Shared with the world? What is missing? What do you want to see on the screen that isn't there yet? What do *you* know that others don't… yet?

It is an exciting, diverse world out there and formats are one of the best ways to show it. They reflect the world we live in. If there's something you want to see on screen that isn't there, why wait for anyone else to develop it?

Get out there and create the next hit format.

Appendix
Development Circle Exercises

The outline of each exercise is set out here so you can follow your progress round the Development Circle.

Chapter 1

Getting Your Eye In – Chapter 1 encourages you to start practising analysing formats that already exist.

Chapter 2

Flipping Modes – this exercise at the end of Chapter 2 encourages you to use your senses to become focused on your surroundings, and then to allow your thoughts to wander, whilst taking notes in both modes to develop an awareness of your own habits of thought.

Chapter 3

TEASER – the grid laid out in Chapter 3 guides you through ideas generation to find your hook or insights.
Practice Makes Perfect – in the same chapter this exercise has you apply all the TEASER questions to pre-existing formats.

Chapter 4

Start at the End – the clearest way to work out which of the story shapes discussed in Chapter 4 will work for your idea is to think about your ending.
Where in the World – starting to sketch out the setting for your story through simple choices.
Who's in Control? – this exercise helps you think about how tightly controlled the action is versus leaving room for reaction.
What's the Trajectory? – exploring how the story might be segmented across single episodes or series.
Yes, but What Is It *Really* about? – the last exercise in Chapter 4 circles around the hook or insight from the TEASER Grid one more time in light of some of those big decisions.

Chapter 5

Stepping-Stones – this exercise in Chapter 5 encourages you to list the action stepping-stones that will get you to the grand finale.

Act Up – start organising your stepping-stones into an act structure.

Finding the Beat –working through the format points to find the beats for action/reaction.

Set the Challenge/Get the Emotion – the Chapter 5 exercises continue by exploring the external challenges set up by the format points, and the internal challenges that will give you the right format beats.

Take the Strain – find the inherent tension in your story and build on it, heighten it and make sure your format points are all pulling things in the right direction.

Chapter 6

Getting Your Eye In (Again) – Chapter 6 begins by taking you back to the very first exercise but this time with a particular focus on the sights and sounds, as well as pace and "energy".

How Special Is "Special"? – this exercise goes back around **Where in the World** and the **Stepping-Stones** exercises to think in more detail about where they sit in a reality/fantasy continuum and how you might choose to enhance them in either direction.

Striking the Right Note – making use of you notes from **Getting Your Eye In (Again)** to practice articulating the "tone" of a show and examining how the design elements contribute to that.

Set the Code – your story world will also embody a set of values and this Chapter 6 exercise asks how that works with your tone and hook.

Detail It and Style It Out – some important questions that take you into more of the specific detail of how your style and tone might be realised in tangible form.

The One and Only – practice spotting the "iconic" moments in formats, and then considering where they might come from in your own format idea.

Change Your Tune? – the final exercise in Chapter 6 pushes you to list the usual ways of doing your topic (focus mode), and then to try out the design opposites for size (spontaneous mode).

Chapter 7

Hero of the Hour? – Chapter 7's first exercise asks you to link your driving question from the TEASER Grid to the question of "who". Who will want to answer that question?

Opposing Forces? – taking in account your protagonist and the driving question of the story, this exercise considers the "forces of antagonism" that must be overcome.

Three and Three – this exercise ensures you link the function of your characters, using Greimas's terminology, back to your format points or **Stepping-Stones** and the three-act structure detailed in Chapter 5's **Act Up**.

Who Is Invited? – thinking about the story world participants again, but now starting to see them from a casting point of view, that is, skills and attributes and includes a diversity sense check.

A Class Act – takes you through some of the possibilities in terms of professional talent and the roles they might play.

What's My Motivation? – the last exercise in Chapter 7 explores what the motivations for non-professional participants might be, bearing in mind they are the ones who must answer your driving question.

Chapter 8

Know Your Drivers – In Chapter 8, the focus now switches back to you once again, as this exercise encourages you to think about the values that drive you.

Team Goldilocks – is your "ideas team" too big, too small or just right?

IWISHU – this figure demonstrates ways of reframing unsatisfactory situations into more useful questions.

Staying Positive – this exercise encourages you to frame conversations in a way that will help you get constructive criticism on a challenging idea.

Pitching Checklist – this exercise takes you through some of the essentials of pitching and reminding you of your path through the Development Circle.

Index

10 Years Younger 48, 50

actant 93, 94, 99
active imagination 18
act structure 64–69
agency 20, 55, 59, 80, 96, 104, 106
All Together Now 31
antagonist 96–98
The Apprentice 68, 70, 88, 95
arcs 59–60, 63–64, 95, 106, 127
Archer, William 66
archetypes 17, 42, 93, 94
Aristotle 66, 67, 75, 93; *see also* act structure
Art of the Thought 13, 24–25; *see also* Wallas, Graham
audience 4, 33, 34, 42, 72, 84, 102, 120–122

Bake Off: The Professionals 102
Bargain Hunt 86, 105
Barthes, Roland 42–43
Baumgartner Restoration 49, 51
Bazalgette, Peter 6, 33, 34
Big Brother 6, 7, 47, 57, 86, 97
de Bono, Edward 26–27, 30, 31; *see also* lateral thinking
Booker, Christopher 43, 78
brain networks 19; *see also* neuroscience
brainstorming 26, 31–32, 33, 124; *see also* Osborn, Alex
brief 27–28; *see also* commissioning
budget 31, 98, 117, 123–124, 128
Butler, Nell; *see also Come Dine with Me*

Campbell, Joseph 42, 43, 78, 93; *see also* hero's journey
casting 3, 10, 91, 102–104; *see also* character, participants

cause and effect 26, 64, 67, 70, 119; *see also* narrative, story
Chalaby, Jean 4, 6, 7
change formats 48–49, 50, 61, 84, 88, 95, 98
Changing Rooms 48, 50
character 9, 42, 54, 70; definition 92–94; types 94–99; *see also* antagonist, participant roles, protagonist
Chion, Michel 87
choice formats 49, 52, 54, 70, 95, 98, 105
The Circle 7
collaboration 31, 111–112
colour 9, 30, 78, 87–88, 90
Come Dine with Me 9, 29, 32, 33, 44, 47, 56, 60, 75, 84, 101
commissioner 27–28, 36, 90, 110, 116–118, 120–121, 123
competition formats 44–48, 48, 54, 61, 63, 74, 95, 105, 128
contributors *see* participant roles
convergent thinking 14, 25–26, 37; *see also* divergent thinking, Guilford, J.P., Structure of Intellect
Costello, Gerard 37, 55, 67, 82, 119, 121, 128; *see also Location, Location Location*
creativity 3, 12–14, 21, 124; Four C Model 13, 18, 31, 115; *see also* creative process, neuroscience, psychological types
creative climate 112–113
creative leadership 112–115
creative process 24–39; *see also* brainstorming, convergent thinking, divergent thinking, lateral thinking

Dancing on Ice 47
Development Circle x–xi, 1–3, 8, 27, 41, 102, 118, 126–128, 130
diegesis *see* story world

134 Index

Dietrich, Arne 3, 20, 22; see also neuroscience
Dirty Dancing: The Time of Your Life 72
divergent thinking 14, 20, 25–26, 30, 37; see also convergent thinking, Guilford, J.P., Structure of Intellect
DIY SOS: The Big Build 48, 99
The Dog House 121
Dragon's Den ix, 34, 53, 54, 60, 67–68, 74, 84, 87, 95, 96, 101, 106

Eating with my Ex 58
ego 15, 17, 94; see also Jung, C. G., psychological types
endings 54, 65, 66, 67, 75, 98, 123
Ex on the Beach 36, 38, 58, 63, 79, 88
experts 70, 80, 87, 97, 100, 112
Extraordinary Extensions 50
extrovert 15–16; see also psychological types

Faking It 7, 8
Family Fortunes 95
fantasy 13, 18, 55, 79, 80, 89, 131; see also realism
Farmer Wants a Wife 29
feedback 111, 114, 115–116, 125
Field, Syd 64, 66
First Dates 29, 32, 34, 38, 39, 42, 52, 56, 58, 60, 79, 80, 96, 103, 104, 105
Formats: definition 6–9; history 3–6; super formats 6; three paradoxes 8, 20, 42, 43, 44, 56–57, 63, 69, 78, 89, 91–92; tight/loose; see also agency; types see competition, change, and choice formats
format points 59, 64–65, 70, 74, 77, 80, 87, 127
format beats 58, 69–71, 73, 75, 82, 91, 96, 101
Four in a Bed 47

gameshows 4, 56, 59, 96, 104
genre 7, 9, 43–44
Glow Up: Britain's Next Make-Up Star 46
The Great British Bake Off 1, 5, 9, 27, 46, 56, 58, 79, 84, 86, 87
The Great British Sewing Bee 104
The Great Pottery Throw Down 46
Greimas, A.J. 93, 94, 99
Ground Force 33, 34, 38, 48
Gogglebox 7, 54, 107

Guilford, J.P. 14, 25–26, 37; see also convergent thinking, divergent thinking, Structure of Intellect

Hero's Journey 42, 78, 93; see also Campbell, Joseph
Hill, Annette 7, 44
The Hit List 101
hook 9, 32–39, 44, 46, 50, 52, 60, 103, 115–116, 123
Horace 66
How Clean is Your House 50
Hunted 35, 38, 39, 56, 58, 79, 119

iconography 88, 127
ideas see creative process
ideas team 111–112
I'm a Celebrity: Get Me out of Here 47, 71
intellectual property 4, 5–6
Interior Design Masters 46, 61, 71, 98
influence 39, 113
introvert 15–16; see also psychological types
The Island with Bear Grylls 35, 46, 73, 105
I Survived a Zombie Apocalypse 89

judges 71, 84, 98, 100–101
Jung, C. G. 14–18, 93–94; see also archetypes, active imagination, ego, introvert/extrovert, psychological types, unconscious

The Krypton Factor 4

Lajos, Egri 92
Lambert, Stephen 7, 11, 28, 54, 91, 103, 107, 116, 118, 120, 123
lateral thinking 26; see also de Bono, Edward
Location, Location, Location 8, 37, 38, 39, 49, 52, 67, 70, 80, 82, 95, 99, 106, 121
Love in the Countryside 29
Love in the Flesh 63, 79
Love Island 47, 63, 69, 78, 86, 95

Margolin, Uri 92; see also character
Mary Queen of Shops 49, 51
The Masked Singer 47, 84, 86
Masterchef 3, 9, 46, 56, 83, 86, 101, 102, 104
Mastermind 47
McKee, Robert 43, 70, 71, 96; see also antagonist, format beats

McKerrow, Richard 27, 29, 56, 57, 79, 81, 84, 97, 111, 118; *see also The Great British Bake Off*
Meenagh, Jonathan 31, 35, 45, 58, 60, 72, 73, 97, 106, 119; *see also Hunted, The Island with Bear Grylls*
mimesis 79
Minhas, Narinder 30, 31, 81, 89, 103, 104, 111, 112, 118; *see also Take a Hike*
The Minimalists: Less Is Now 48, 50
mise-en-scène 85–88; *see also* style
de Moraes, Ana 29, 32, 34, 42, 60, 77, 103, 104, 108, 109, 116, 117, 121; *see also First Dates*
motivation 104–107
Myers-Briggs test 17
My Mechanic 49, 51

Naked, Alone and Racing to Get Home 36, 40
Naked Attraction 2, 34, 49, 52, 56, 86, 99
Naked Beach 29
narrative 7, 8, 41–43, 59, 66, 69, 73, 92, 102; *see also* cause and effect, protagonist, story
narrator 87, 101, 102, 107, 120
neuroscience 19–20, 24
Ninja Warrior UK 47, 56, 104

One Born Every Minute 34, 35
Osborn, Alex 26, 30, 31; *see also* brainstorming

participants 58–59, 74, 82, 86, 87, 91, 96, 97, 100–102, 105, 120; *see also* agency, casting, character
pass/fail device 45, 72
Phillips, Kate 32, 63, 75, 88, 102
pitching 116–124
Pointless 47, 82, 104
Pop Idol 6
presenters 60, 82, 83, 87, 99, 101–102
Propp, Vladimir 42, 59, 93, 94, 98; *see also* character, story
protagonist 7, 72, 94–96, 97, 98, 100, 120
psychological types 15–17

Queer Eye 9, 50, 56, 95
quiz shows 4, 45, 47, 59, 66, 75, 78, 82, 95, 96, 101, 104, 105, 106

Race Across the World 7, 9, 36, 56, 78, 86, 95

Ramsay's Kitchen Nightmares 49, 51, 95
realism 78–81; *see also* fantasy
The Repair Shop 49, 51, 56, 60, 68, 73
resilience 108–111, 126
The Restoration Man 48, 50, 51, 84–85
reveals 72–73, 75, 127
Roseman, Caroline 33, 36, 58, 59, 70, 72, 74, 88, 102, 118, 119, 122; *see also Ex on the Beach*
RuPaul's Drag Race 1, 95

SAS: Who Dares Wins 45, 46, 57, 72, 73, 86, 89, 95, 101, 105
segmentation 120
setting 10, 56–57, 86; *see also* story world
Sort Your Life Out with Stacey Solomon
sound 77, 85, 87–88
story 41–54, 59–61, 63–64, 118, 119, 122; driver *see* hooks; stepping-stones 65, 69, 71, 77, 127; story beats *see* format beats; *see also* act structure, antagonist, arc, cause and effect, format beats, format points, narrative, protagonist
story world 9, 48, 55, 57, 66, 78–81; *see also* diegesis, setting, style
Strictly Come Dancing 1, 9, 47, 56, 57, 73, 80, 83, 88, 100, 101, 102
Structures of Intellect 25; *see also* divergent thinking, convergent thinking, Guilford, J.P.
style 77, 81, 85, 87, 88; *see also mise en scène*
Supernanny 48

Take a Hike 30, 47, 56, 60, 84, 89, 103, 104
Tattoo Fixers 1, 50
TEASER 32–39, 55, 61, 110, 115
tension 44–45, 46, 50, 52, 70, 71, 72, 73–74; *see also* act structure, antagonist, format points, format beats, hooks
Tidying Up with Marie Kondo 48
tone 77, 81–83, 88, 90, 102, 117, 119, 122; *see also* style, values
Top Gear 115–116
Total Wipeout 88

unconscious 14–15, 17–18, 22, 79
Undercover Boss 7, 53
University Challenge 47

values 81, 83–85, 90, 98, 107, 109–111
Vogler, Christopher 43

The Voice 47, 57, 84, 88, 104
Vonnegut, Kurt 43

Wallas, Graham 13, 24, 25, 37; *see also Art of Thought*, creative process
What Not to Wear 48, 50
Wheeler Dealers 61, 68, 100

Who Wants to be a Millionaire 5, 6, 9, 66, 82
Wife Swap 7, 28

The X Factor 47

Yorke, John 64
You Are What You Eat 48